Paul Tillich's
Radical Social Thought

Paul Tillich's Radical Social Thought

RONALD H. STONE

John Knox Press
ATLANTA

230.09
T465Ys

80112020

Library of Congress Cataloging in Publication Data

Stone, Ronald H
    Paul Tillich's radical social thought.

    Includes bibliographical references and index.
    1. Tillich, Paul, 1886–1965 2. Religion and
sociology—History. I. Title
BX4827.T53S76   261.8′092′4   79–87740
ISBN 0–8042–0679–1

© copyright John Knox Press 1980
10 9 8 7 6 5 4 3 2 1
Printed in the United States of America
John Knox Press
Atlanta, Georgia 30308

Christopher Alan
June 22–July 4, 1972

Preface

The impact of Paul Tillich on North American theology and religious life is widely acknowledged. The connections between his theology and political life are less appreciated. In the final quarter of the twentieth century, the inquiry into the systematic relationship between the religious foundations of a culture and the political life of a culture has received a fresh impetus. It is widely recognized that a rupture between the religious convictions of a people and the practical politics of their governors is a disaster. The dangers of the political processes of the present, which result in the threats of meaninglessness, nuclear war, starvation, and brutal dictatorships, drive sensitive people to ask again about the relationship of their faith to their practice. The twentieth century has turned away from the realistic balance of power struggles of the nineteenth century toward ideological struggles expressed in the wars against Nazism and Fascism, in the ongoing struggles between Communism and Capitalism, Catholic and Protestant in Northern Ireland, Hindu and Moslem on the Indian subcontinent, and Jew and Moslem in the Holy Land, and in the wars of liberation in the third world. The religious dimension of these struggles is more obvious than the religious resources for reconciliation.

As a student of religion and politics, I am driven to inquire into theories of religion and politics that will help us synthesize our political practice with our deepest religious loyalties. Paul Tillich is a particularly good teacher in this respect. For half a century he thought about the relationship of religion and society. Much of his thought about society has been neglected, because it was published in German in the interwar struggles of the Weimar period. He won his influence in the United States as a theologian, and his role as a social philosopher was neglected by Americans. Only recently (1977) has his major work in social philosophy, *The Socialist Decision,* been translated; and many of his other German works on social questions remain untranslated. Americans have written doctoral dissertations on his German socialist work, but these studies have neglected his work on social philosophy in the United States. To date, no one else has undertaken to present an interpretation of the riches of his total social thought.

Tillich became important for me as a beginning theological student in 1960 at Union Theological Seminary. His thought provided an intelligible understanding of Christian faith even though his German idealist-existentialist heritage was different from my own. In my second year at Union, Alfred North Whitehead's process philosophy came to play a similar role of grounding faith in an intelligible ontology. Later, as I studied social philosophy, the thought of Reinhold Niebuhr provided a developed Christian perspective on the political-social struggles of contemporary society. After a decade of social activism and the teaching of social philosophy to Protestant theological students, I became impressed once again with the thought of Paul Tillich. From Niebuhr I had learned of the social importance of the political thought of Augustine, Thomas, and Calvin. So when I once again picked up Tillich it was with new eyes. Now I could see him as a theologian, but as a theologian driven to answer theoretical questions about social practice.

I found in Tillich a radical social thinker. He pushed questions about the theory of society to their depths. The power of a political concept was finally grounded in the adequacy of its correspondence to the actual human situation in both its existence and its essence. Questions of social theory could finally be related or correlated to answers with theological depth.

Often his thought was also radical in a secondary sense. It was radical in that it affirmed revolution. In a capitalist world, he was a socialist. But this meaning of radical is secondary; more important is the radicalness of his probing that pushes to the roots of the human condition in society. He unmasked the pretensions of the societies in which he lived, and he revealed the personal substance of self which inclined his social philosophy to take the shape it realized.

His social thought is rooted in the society and the self. The self, society, and thought are all in time, and all evolve as the new events of history impinge upon them. So his social philosophy is understandable only in the context of his life in society. I have tried to provide enough of the story of his life and times to explicate the social theory without providing a full biography of his life. The first volume, *Life,* of the biography by Wilhelm and Marion Pauck, *Paul Tillich: His Life and Thought,* appeared while this study was in process. This work has benefited from it, but the different perspective on Tillich the social philosopher will be clear to readers of both volumes.

James Luther Adams was immensely helpful to me in the early stages of my research in the Tillich archives at the Harvard Divinity School. Professors John Stumme and James V. Fisher have both contributed to my understanding of Tillich through conversation and their written works. The research at Harvard could not have been undertaken without the invitation of the Harvard Faculty to spend a sabbatical there as a Visiting Scholar. Mr. Peter Oliver, former librarian of the Harvard Divinity School, was most helpful in assisting me in the use of the Harvard Archives. I want to thank Dr. Robert C. Kimball, executor of the literary estate of Paul Tillich, for permission to use and to quote from the archival materials. The Program Agency of the United Presbyterian Church, USA, and the Association of Theological Schools provided funds for the research. The Pittsburgh Theological Seminary graciously provided sabbatical leaves in the fall terms of 1975 and 1978, which provided the time and the primary means of support for the study. The typing of the manuscript has been competently and kindly done by Priscilla Boyd and Terri Treemarcki, secretaries at the seminary. Marian G. Lord has greatly improved the manuscript by her superb copyediting.

Grateful acknowledgement is made to:

Dr. Robert C. Kimball, Executor, Literary Estate of Paul Tillich, for permission to quote from the Tillich Archive at the Andover-Harvard Theological Library of the Harvard Divinity School.

Union Seminary Quarterly Review for permission to use in chapter 7 the content of my essay "Tillich's Critical Use of Marx and Freud in the Social Context of the Frankfort School," which appeared in Fall, 1977.

Religion in Life for permission to use in chapter 8 my essay "Tillich: Radical Political Theologian," which appeared in Spring, 1977.

Paul Tillich's Radical Social Thought

Paul Tillich's
Radical Social Thought

I.
The Origins

The search for the roots of Paul Tillich's social philosophy takes one to Berlin. There on an afternoon in late August I stood in the Potsdamer Platz and watched the wind blow newspapers across the uncut grass of the desolate, divided square that had been the center of the administrated terror of the Third Reich. I remembered Paul Tillich's vision before the Nazi take-over, a vision of sheep grazing in a forsaken Potsdamer Platz, which at that time was the cultural-political heart of Berlin. After the war he returned to Berlin, and the sheep were there eating the weeds.

A few minutes walk from Potsdamer Platz the ruins of the Kaiser Wilhelm Memorial Church stand as a reminder that the origins of Tillich's social thought reach back beyond Nazi Germany through the Weimar Republic to imperial Germany. Here at the church Tillich, going into exile, cursed the Nazis and the German Christians from a perspective formed in a different Germany. He cursed them as one raised in the Germany of the empire, as a son of the Weimar Republic, but with the earthiness and gusto of a Martin Luther in the sixteenth century.

The quest for the forces that molded the person of Paul Tillich has taken Renate Albrecht and Gertraut Stöber to Poland to visit the childhood sites of the young Paul.[1] There they have found that most of the Germans who lived in the towns of Starzeddel, the birthplace, and Bad Schonfliess, Königsberg, and Butterfelde, the scenes of his childhood, have emigrated to be replaced by Poles. The house in which Tillich was born on August 20, 1886, in Starzeddel is now a Roman Catholic rectory, and the thirteenth-century Romanesque church of which Tillich's father was an Evangelical pastor is once again a Roman Catholic church.

The visit to Königsberg revealed that the Friedrich-Wilhelm Gymnasium, which Tillich attended for two years as a boy, had been destroyed by the war and that in fact Königsberg, now called Koina in Polish, had been largely destroyed. Bad Schonfliess, Tillich's residence from 1891 to 1898, remains true to his later-day memories of it as an enchanted garden, a minor town surrounded by a medieval wall that seemed to be created for children to walk on as they fantasized of feudal times and dreamed of their futures.

Butterfelde, the scene of Tillich's first romance, engagement, and marriage in 1913, still is full of sites marking the young Tillich's courtship of Grethi Wever. The former Wever estate is now a state-run enterprise. The town itself is drab and in need of repair; but at the lake and the church with its cemetery, memories of the past remain.

Here in these towns and villages Paul Tillich grew up in imperial Germany in the nineteenth century. He rested secure in the love of his mother, Mathilde Durseln Tillich, and under the protective guidance of his father, Johannes Tillich, a leading Lutheran pastor.

Paul Tillich has written his own memory of his childhood in several places. His own myth of his origin is not substantially questioned by any of the considerable outside data now available, and so his own story tells us much about the social forces that made Tillich the person he was.

The origins of his social thought rest in the human reality of the person. He is first shaped by his family, society, and education. His religion is given to him in these institutions as well as in the church. Tillich reflects critically upon his society as he and it are broken in World War I, and in his need he turns to socialist theory as a body of ideas for understanding the social crisis. His thought uses critically the sources of his life and finds that socialist theory shares some of

those same sources. Paul Tillich is a very autobiographical philosopher. He thinks out of the conflicts of his own life and time. This
fact is perhaps more obvious in his social philosophy than in his
philosophy of religion.

Family

Tillich's reflections on his family credit his parents with combining the temperaments of eastern and western Germany. His father
contributed meditative inclinations with a soberness and a strong
sense of duty and authority. His mother, on the other hand, was
more representative of the sensuous mobility and democratic tendencies of the Rhineland.[2] His father, as a Lutheran pastor and
school superintendent, was a Prussian servant of the state with all
that connoted in the late nineteenth century. Throughout his life
Tillich would combine respect for authority and deference to offi-
cials with his own longing for ecstasy. In his autobiography, *On the
Boundary,* he admits to the prevalence of extreme Dionysiac tendencies in himself, which were in tension with the Apollonarian life he
chose as a minister and professor in Germany.

The family provided the context for the successful passage
through the stages of childhood.[3] The birth trauma, highlighted as
of utmost importance in the Pauck biography,[4] seems to have been
navigated, and by his seventeenth birthday he had developed into
a basically trustful individual. He, of course, was subject to the
normal social repressions imposed on pretheological students who
were sons of outstanding Lutheran pastors. His attempts at overthrowing tradition would always be accompanied by guilt, but the
courage rooted in his basic trust enabled him to accept the guilt and
continue the challenge. Groomed to be among the academic elite,
his industry was prodigious, and yet he knew areas in which his
knowledge was not complete. While Tillich was working out his
identity, his mother died at the young age of forty-three.

Rollo May, Tillich's close friend and biographer, has brought his
training in psychoanalysis to bear upon Tillich's reaction to his
mother's death. If May is right that she was the power in the home

and that Paul had not yet resolved his sexual fantasies about her, the impact of her premature death could have deepened the identity crisis. So it did as Tillich was driven to confront meaning and non-meaning. In his grief he wrote:

> Am I then I? who tells me that I am!
> Who tells me what I am, what I shall become?
> What is the world's and what life's meaning?
> What is being and passing away on earth?
>
> O abyss without ground, dark depth of madness!
> Would that I had never gazed upon you and were
> sleeping like a child![5]

The influence of Hamlet upon the young boy approaching manhood was unmistakable. He involved the death of his mother in his struggle for identity, searched himself, and in courage prepared to enter the university the next year.

May suggests that some of Tillich's secretiveness with women and his passionate search for their love reflect issues that the early death of his mother left unresolved.[6] It also left him exposed to the conflicts with his father without his mother's comfort. There is no doubt that his father, the examiner of theological students in philosophy for the Brandenburg Consistory, represented a stern ideal to emulate. Their correspondence, however, shows a warmth and a mutual understanding. The hard conflicts would not surface until the younger Tillich had started the critique of his tradition after the war. In his autobiography, Tillich himself is sensitive to the insight that his struggle against traditional authority is rooted in his struggle with his patriarchal father. His affirmation of autonomy, or freedom, over against heteronomy, or outside control, is both an affirmation of the modern age and of his own liberation. Tillich fought the "Grand Inquisitor" throughout his life and remained sensitive to its reappearance in religious life.

Tillich's younger sisters, Johanna and Elisabeth, found themselves admiringly following their elder brother. The persuasiveness of the religiousness of the family is witnessed to by the fact that they both married young ministers. (Emmanuel Hirsch, Tillich's boyhood friend and bitter theological-political opponent in the thirties, was passed over by Johanna in her choice of Alfred Fritz. The Paucks report that Hirsch's grief was very severe.[7])

Society

From our perspective the Hohenzollern dynasty, which was sitting so comfortably on the thrones of Prussia and the empire in the nineteenth century, was doomed. The Romanovs, Hapsburgs, and Hohenzollerns were all destined to be thrown aside by World War I. Paul Tillich was a child of the empire: his father accompanied the imperial party to Jerusalem, and the Tillichs had frequent contact with minor nobility. Under Wilhelm II (1890–1918), state, church, and army were unified in a *Kultur-religion.* Wilhelm II's proclamation, "One Kingdom, one people, one God," suggests the truth. There was a cultural uneasiness that would pour forth its sickness in the Weimar Republic's failure, but the progressive forces were not united against the kaiser. People, religion, and the institutions of the monarchy, including the army, functioned to keep the tensions of industrial society repressed until 1914.

The Germany united by Bismarck in 1871 was going through rapid industrial expansion. The strains of this expansion were reflected in the alienation of the rapidly increasing industrial working class in the Ruhr, Berlin, and the new industrial cities in conditions. The suffering of the workers was reduced by the social legislation of Bismarck, but their alienation from the establishment of German court and church grew. Despite counterattacks from the ruling class, membership in the unions increased and the Social Democratic party grew—even though divided between liberals and radicals—in the later nineteenth century. Germany, during Tillich's early years of 1886–1914, was in a prerevolutionary state that required defeat in war and economic collapse to unleash the revolution.

The rise of Prussia had encouraged the ideologies of anti-Semitism, *Realpolitik,* and reactionary nationalism.[8] Tillich himself was untouched by these movements, but his commitments to the church of his father and his vocational choice involved him unconsciously in the support of the traditional relationship of the Junkers and the peasants. The monarchy deferred to the special interests of the Junkers east of the Elbe, and the Evangelical church, as the monarch's church, supported the arrangement with its emphasis upon docility among the people and its focus on respect for hierarchies. Tillich's own memories of his boyhood stress an awareness of the class divisions. Though he played among the children of the common school, his father's position and contacts and his own move into the gymnasium (academic high school) set him apart from his playmates.

Prewar Berlin in its political functioning shielded the alliance of the old Junker class with the conservative capitalist interests under the pomp and panoply of monarchy. Equipped with a religious reinforcement of vocation, the Prussian bureaucracy rationalized life and assured itself that all was well despite the rumblings of malcontents. Despite the religious self-consciousness of much of the establishment, Berlin was secularizing itself in its expansion as fewer workers took the church seriously and as the church's thought was defeated in the academic market place. Ernst Troeltsch's picture of a church unsure of its mission fits the Evangelical church of the Tillichs. Similarly, politics was constituted on an inadequate basis. Max Weber saw the confusion. Autocracy ruled over a parliamentary sham. The Junkers were declining economically, and their rule was dangerous. The middle class was too immature to rule and too inclined to seek a leader; and, of course, the proletariat lacked the training and experience for rule. The political base was a premonition of disaster.[9]

The monarchy was a symbol of the patriarchy that characterized Tillich's Germany. After the war there was a time of the rebellion of the sons—and in socialism some recognition of the rights of the daughters—but prewar Germany was the father's world with everything in place for the establishment fathers.

Tillich's society and his early ministry from 1912 to 1914 in the working section of Berlin revealed to him the alienation of the industrial worker. His social philosophy, as it developed in the Weimar Republic, however, would never be freed from the memory of Germany's feudal past. His socialism would never be simply the intellectual's portrayal of the industrial worker's needs because he knew personally the shock of the rural person's migration to the city. But distinct from the proletariat, his life would alternate between rural and urban life. His life was not exclusively in the city; his opportunity was in the city, but he had his rural escapes.

University

After graduation from the Friedrich-Wilhelm Gymnasium in 1904, the year after his mother's death, Tillich registered in theological studies in Berlin. In a typical program of study for an Evangelical pastoral-academic career, he studied at Tübingen and, more importantly, at Halle from 1905 to 1907. He fulfilled the expectations of his ecclesiastical superiors in the Brandenburg Consistory and passed his theological examinations in 1909 and 1912. In August, 1912, he was ordained in the Evangelical Church of the Prussian Union, which was a united church containing both Lutherans and Calvinists. He had received his Ph.D. in Breslau in 1910 and his licentiate in theology (the highest degree awarded in theology at that time) from Halle in 1911.

Tillich has left a valuable record of his university years in a letter he wrote to fellow refugee Thomas Mann on May 23, 1943.[10] Mann had written Tillich requesting details of German theological education in the early 1900s for use in his novel *Doctor Faustus.* [11] The description of much of Adrian Leverkuhn's theological education at Halle is a paraphrase and sometimes exact quotations from Tillich's letter.[12] The professor in *Doctor Faustus,* Ehrenfried Kumpf, is a thinly disguised version of Tillich's most important mentor, Martin Kahler. On the other hand, Mann's lecturer, Eberhard Schleppfus, was a repudiation of the material Tillich had furnished. Tillich had insisted in his letter that there was no literal belief in the Devil at Halle and that he had not heard of demonic-like distortions of the natural in his theological education. Nevertheless, Mann uses Schleppfus in the novel to deepen the association of the fictional theological education and the occult. In fact, even his character of Kumpf is made to represent a primitive belief in a literal Devil that Tillich had assured Mann was absent from Halle.

Theological education was determined by the universities, which were institutions of the state, and then examined by the church. The first years were spent in biblical exegesis and historical studies. Tillich was always proud of his ability in Latin and Greek, learned in the gymnasium, and characteristically began lectures with etymological reflections on key terms. His Hebrew, learned at Halle, is used less extensively in his work even when preaching, as he often did, on Old Testament themes. The middle period of theological education was spent in the central studies of systematic theology, philosophy of religion, and ethics. The concluding period, usually the fourth year, was spent in the disciplines of practical theology: homiletics, education, pastoral ministry, etc. The role of philosophy in the curriculum depended on the outlook of the particular school. Tillich emphasized philosophy and became a lifelong friend with Fritz Medicus, the young lecturer from Halle. Medicus deserves the primary credit for the thorough instruction the young Tillich received in German idealism. This influence is reflected in both of Tillich's dissertations on Friedrich Schelling and continues throughout his work to emerge in his *Systematic Theology* and in his lectures on German idealism at Harvard University half a century after his introduction to the tradition at the University of Halle. It is important to recognize the innocence of Paul Tillich from the onslaughts of Kierkegaard, a post–World War I phenomenon; from Nietzsche, discovered by Tillich during the war; and from Marx, studied during the stormy years of the Weimar Republic. Also, there is no evidence of formal instruction in the social problems of contemporary Germany or realization of the need for a theological critique of the complacency of Wilhelmian society.

As a theological student, Tillich found the faculty at Halle divided between the pietists, who emphasized revelation, orthodoxy, and traditional exegesis, and the liberals. The liberals had set to recasting theology in the light of the contemporary historical-critical methodology. Tillich found the liberals carrying the debate on the scholarly level, and they opened his thought to far-reaching skepticism of the literalness of the historical claims of traditional Christianity. In his letter to Mann in 1943, however, he reported that he found the traditional orthodox picture of theological anthropology more persuasive than the liberal optimism, which reflected a bourgeois ideology of progress.[13] The picture Tillich gives us of his student days is that of a student working on his own synthesis of the theological options. He accepted radical historical scholarship, but sought to expound the meaning of traditional theological concepts in terms of an adequate metaphysic.[14] In his efforts to reestablish metaphysics, he distinguishes his work from the Ritschlian theology that tried to ground Christian faith almost entirely on ethical insight and value philosophy. The concrete meaning of this distinction is best seen in his dissertations on Schelling.

Contributing to the socialization and identity of the young Tillich was the Wingolf Society. Tillich joined this fraternity of students at Halle and rose to the role of first officer in its ranks. He remembered with devotion the friendships, conversations, and comradeship he found in the society. For Tillich the group did not serve the spirit of adolescent rebellion that it did for many of his contemporaries. It was the fraternity of his father, with whom he kept up a lively correspondence about the society, and the older Tillich continued to participate in its affairs as an elder member.

Tillich honored the asceticism of the society regarding sex; but, according to the Paucks, the liberalism of the group regarding alcoholic beverages increased under his leadership. In the disputes about the Christian foundation of the national organization, Tillich argued on the orthodox side for keeping its Christian principles dominant.

Tillich's philosophical brilliance and personal presence attracted respect and even awe in the society. His need for a group of friends came into its own in the Wingolf (friendship house) and here he formed his lasting friendships with Hermann Schaft, Alfred Fritz, and Heinrich Meinhof. Characteristically, for the remainder of his career, he worked with a group of friends, sharing his insights first in conversation.

The Wingolf Society was a Christian fellowship and nondueling fraternity, but the pictures of Tillich with the fraternity or in small groups of his fraternal brothers show the full martial spirit of the organization. He is dressed in the uniform of the society complete with plumed hat, dress sword, sash, and black leather boots. Again, the society reveals the origins of Tillich in prewar Germany as he lived in the *Kulturreligion* of academic-Lutheran monarchism.[15]

II.
Friedrich Schelling

As a university student, Paul Tillich learned from Kant, Fichte, and Hegel, but the primary source of his thought was Friedrich Schelling (1775–1854). As mentioned earlier, Fritz Medicus, the Fichte scholar, initiated him into German idealism at Halle. During the period 1909–1912, while an assistant pastor and student, Tillich developed his work on Schelling. He recorded his excitement upon finding his own copies of Schelling's writings:

> I recall the unforgettable moment when by chance I came into possession of the very rare first edition of the collected works of Schelling in a bookstore on my way to the University of Berlin. I had no money, but I bought it anyway, and this spending of nonexistent money was probably more important than all the other nonexistent or sometimes existing money that I have spent. *For what I learned from Schelling became determinative of my own philosophical and theological development.* [1] (Emphasis added.)

Tillich has often confessed his dependence upon the work of Schelling. In his old age in the forward to his *Gesammelte Werke,* [2] he indicated that the writings of others had made him aware of his continued reliance upon concepts of Schelling, though he himself had not investigated the dominance of his Schelling studies upon his later work.

The two dissertations Tillich wrote on Schelling were formative of his thought. Later years enriched his ideas, but the basic formulations drawn from Schelling were maintained. Schelling's ontology underlies the political philosophy of the later Tillich even though Schelling's particular political ideas were neglected. The translator of the dissertations, Victor Nuovo, has observed:

> It is as though the principles of Schelling's later philosophy, as they are presented by Tillich in these early works, found a place at the very roots of his consciousness and determined all his future thought.[3]

Schelling's early enthusiasm for the French Revolution and his activity as a leader of the Tübingen radicals in the 1790s had no direct political influence on Tillich, who found in him a metaphysical not a political guide. The early hopes of Schelling, Hölderlin, and Hegel that a change in consciousness would produce political change[4] seem not to be reflected in Tillich's work on the philosophy of the later, more apolitical Schelling. Tillich's political innocence at the time of his dissertations prevented him from analyzing the political consequences of Schelling's philosophy of freedom.

History of Religion

The dissertation presented to the University of Breslau for the doctor's degree in philosophy, *The Construction of the History of Religion in Schelling's Positive Religion,* was published in 1910. It is breathtaking in scope as in the first part it explains the concept of the potencies, which is the key to Schelling's metaphysic. The implications of the doctrine of the potencies for God, man, and world are then expounded. In the second part of the dissertation, Tillich surveys the history of religion as it has evolved in Schelling's perspective from prehistoric time to the development of the church. In the third part, the implications of all of the foregoing for the philosophies of history and religion are explicated.

The potencies are Schelling's most basic concept. They are very full, drawing material from the history of religion, metaphysics, theology, and the philosophy of nature. "The first potency is nonbeing, $\mu\dot{\eta}$ ov."[5] It is that which comes to be, and it is the ground of the unconscious. The first potency is expressed in the doctrine of God, in the analysis of the world, and in human nature. Tillich first traces the development of the idea of the potencies in Schelling and then explains them in his later philosophy. The intuition of the potencies in being is based upon the reality necessary to produce the free spirit in humanity. The first potency is the lack of being, and the second is the fullness of being. In the first potency that which will be is purely potential, in the second it is purely act. Both of the potencies are incomplete. The third potency is a combination of the first two in both subject and object and is free to be.[6]

The concern of Schelling's *On the Nature of Human Freedom* was to interpret the freedom of humanity, and for Schelling this meant that freedom in God had to be made intelligible. Despite Tillich's repeated assertion that Schelling achieves "perfect clarity" in the doctrine of the potencies, the argument is strange to those not raised in German romantic-idealistic categories.

Tillich's suggestion that the greatest clarity regarding the potencies is found in Schelling's doctrine of God should be taken seriously, and the suggestion also implies Tillich's failure to render them clearly in the tortuous exposition of them in the first section of the thesis. The potencies represent the process of self-realization whether that be in God, the world, or humanity and posit the underlying identity with distinctions of all three. The unity of the nature of God, world, and humanity reveals traces of Jacob Böhme's theosophical thought and its roots in medieval alchemy.

The potencies represent the trinitarian structure of God. Tillich's God as eternal is being itself, but being itself is free to contradict itself, and this is done in the positing, through will, of the world. Humanity as spirit is free from the world like God and is God's link to the world and ultimately to Himself. The positing of the world is the act of the unconscious ground, or the Fall. Humanity also posits itself outside of God in freedom and is consequently estranged from the fullness of God's being though the structure of God's being remains essentially in humanity but is not simply determinative of humanity's existence.

With the Fall the potencies are distinguished and the unity of the eternal process is violated so that, with time, the potencies become the process of history and represent past, present, and future, or Father, Son, and Spirit. The history of humanity becomes a history of religious confusion through which the eternal process will finally restore the world to itself. The structure of Tillich's systematic theology on philosophical grounds as God, Christ, and Spirit is already implied in this first dissertation as is his passion for finding religious meaning in all of history and his treatment of all religious experience as significant for the Christian theologian.

Tillich's philosophy of being depends upon his use of Schelling's understanding of potencies as his epistemology presupposes Schelling's conception of identity. Tillich's existentialism is grounded in Schelling's existentialist critique of Hegel and in the estrangement of humanity and nature in a world in which the act of creation has separated the potencies. His existentialism corresponds to the later positive philosophy of Schelling and is dependent on Schelling's earlier negative philosophy, because for Tillich, all existentialism is dependent upon an essentialism whether acknowledged or unacknowledged.

Part two of the dissertation surprises readers who thought that only in the later years of his life did Tillich discover the importance of non-Christian religions for Christian theology.[7] Here in fewer than forty pages Tillich expounds Schelling's constructive typology for the history of religion, which uses the doctrine of the potencies as a hermeneutic, or means of interpretation for the vast material. Here, as in Tillich's later work,[8] Buddhism receives special emphasis. The history of religions has advanced beyond Schelling's work —in a sense it had hardly begun in the nineteenth century—and Tillich's own work later moved beyond Schelling. But for philosophical theology, the task remains of interpreting the significance of the vast religious experience of humanity.

The distinctive seeds of Tillich's Christology and Christ as the criterion of all religion including Christianity are found in the closing sections of the history of religion material. The power of rebellious selfhood was sacrificed by Christ, and the potencies reconciled. In Christ the "spiritual personality" of God is revealed.

This, then, is the content of all of history: the work of Christ, namely, to sacrifice his natural being in order to find himself again in spirit and in truth; this is the content of history because it is the essence of Spirit. [9]

Tillich hoped that a free-spiritual, philosophical religion would arise from idealism; that is, the emerging religion would be spiritually free using the material of religion and philosophy as concepts. The freedom would depend only on the act that makes one free, for only the act could be unconditioned.

In part three of the dissertation, Tillich turns to the concepts of religion and history. Schelling had developed various concepts in his movement from a Kantian critical background through Fichte to his own speculative position that could realize the concept of religion within the total system. Religion is a relationship "that is essentially within God."[10] "The pure substance of human consciousness is by nature God-positing."[11] Within human consciousness, the interaction of potencies causes "all the distinctions that find their concrete expression in the actual religions."[12] Kant's reduction of religion to morality is overthrown, and the ground for Schleiermacher's feeling of unconditional dependence is laid. Tillich's own expression of "unconditional concern" reaffirms Schelling's move beyond a simple "subject-object scheme."[13]

In his concluding pages, Tillich defended Schelling against the charge that he had created a new mythology. Revelation, which was central to Schelling's system, was external fact, while the content of revelation was the suprahistorical fact. Schelling's insistence upon the factuality of the Christ overthrew idealism.

Mysticism and Guilt-Consciousness

Tillich set out in his second dissertation to show that Schelling had resolved the conflict between the mystic's intuition of unity with God and the moralist's judgment of human opposition to God. His interpretation of Schelling refused to divide Schelling's work into disconnected periods, but stressed that its greatness depended upon the dialectical working out of problems that arise in one period into solutions in the next period. The problem was given in the title: *Mysticism and Guilt-Consciousness in Schelling's Philosophical Develop-*

ment. [14] The issue was whether or not in general and in Schelling in particular the integrity of the religious life based on consciousness of union with God and ethics could be maintained. "Mysticism is the religious expression for the immediate identity of God and man."[15] "Guilt-consciousness is the religious expression for the absolute contradiction between God and man."[16] Behind the investigation of Schelling's answer was the attack by the neo-Kantians on the mysticism of German theology represented in Böhme, Luther, and Schelling. Could the speculative-mystical interests of a Schelling be held together with the critical thought of a Kant? Or, more existentially for Tillich, could mysticism be grounded in a metaphysical system that was not vulnerable to the attacks of the cold moralism of a Ritschl and his followers?

For Schelling religion was, at its core, the way God loves himself through the free spirit of humanity.[17] There is an identity common to God and humanity and the universe that is the presupposition of the relationship. This presupposition is the essence of religion, but in existence the immediate identity is estranged. The actual history of religions is influenced by that estrangement as the sway of guilt-consciousness is acknowledged. There is identity ideally, and identity is realized in Schelling's philosophy of nature, in his mysticism, and in his esthetic intuition; but in actual existence—the realm of freedom—the rebellion of the ego leads to an estrangement that determines the way people organize their religious life under conditions of morality and guilt.

With the emergence of the philosophy of freedom in *Of Human Freedom,* the philosophy of Schelling is opened to the profound realization that the contradiction of mysticism and guilt-consciousness is resolved in grace. Selfhood was the rebellion, and only by taking on selfhood could God suffer with selves and overcome the contradiction of existence. Communion with God, or the victory of mysticism if you will, is won by the one who annuls himself as self and frees the spirit to emerge. The essence of Christianity for the young Tillich was here in the movement from incarnation to crucifixion and exaltation, or from Jesus to Christ to the Spirit.[18] Identity is won but in the form of a communion that has overcome guilt-consciousness.

From his encounter with Schelling, Tillich preserved much that would have been lost. In addition to many specific insights into metaphysics and method, he took general directions that were determinate for his later work:

(1) He remained persuaded that "the finite is not only finite, but in some dimension it is also infinite and has the divine as its center and ground."[19] (2) Aesthetic intuition is potentially revelatory. (3) The infinite has been present in past periods of history, and their meaning is important for theology. (4) The depths of society and humanity reach into the demonic as well as the divine. (5) Tillich gave Schelling credit for the articulation in his time of the power of the unconscious.[20] (6) The affirmation that theology depended upon philosophy was emphasized in Tillich's second, or theological, dissertation.[21] (7) The need for the unity of essentialism and existentialism is reaffirmed throughout both dissertations. (8) The idealist epistemology, with its dependence on the principle of identity, continued to dominate Tillich's work. (9) The presence of dynamic categories within the divine remained an emphasis of Tillich. (10) Elements of nature-mysticism also characterized Tillich's work and life to the end. (11) The problem of combining human freedom and a transcendent fall Tillich inherited from Schelling, and he continued to labor on it. (12) Hints at the method of correlation are present in Tillich's dissertations; what was speculatively required for Schelling in metaphysics became in Tillich a methodological principle for theology. (13) The theological significance of world religions was also learned from Schelling. (14) From other romanticists, more than Schelling, arose the need for a unified society beyond the competition of bourgeois society.

In summary, the essentialist-existentialist metaphysical theologian with a direction toward a romantic appreciation of art and nature is present in the dissertations. Tillich's philosophy of religion is already implicit in his work on Schelling. What is absent from the dissertations is any significant indication of the direction of his social philosophy. He was still politically naïve. The problem of the state as the integrator of religion, culture, economics, and politics had not yet appeared.

When the social problem appeared in Tillich's consciousness, the wrestling with it would reflect this early work in metaphysics. His writing on power would push the analysis back to the speculation on the potencies. Power in *Love, Power, and Justice* would be the overcoming of nonbeing by being. The struggle in the divine life between the first and second potency, or dynamics and form, was also the issue in society between power and justice. The powers of origin had to encounter the demands of justice to produce a society in which humanity could flourish. The union of ontological speculation and ethics, or mysticism and guilt-consciousness, was necessary for a liberating faith that would not disappear under the pressures of the social crisis. Existential awareness of the social struggle, however, would only come in the breakdown of Europe in world war. .

III.
World War I

The thought of Paul Tillich is like a bridge joining the nineteenth century to the twentieth century. The bridge was deeply scarred by the heavy artillery of World War I, as his mind was marked by exploding shells, bayonet charges, the numbing cold, the eternal mud, and the massive dying of his comrades in arms. The mind sought relief from the torture of battle by two serious breakdowns, but the mind held. The nineteenth century ended in World War I, 1914–1918, but in Tillich's thought it continues into the twentieth. The inheritance of the idealist-imperialist German who entered World War I is still present in the realist-democratic American of the post–World War II period.

Chaplain in Combat

He entered the war with a mixture of romantic-religious-nationalist motives. He did not anticipate that the war would interrupt for long his chosen profession of professor or stand in the way of his recent marriage. His training had been idealist and theoretical and his inclinations conservative, though he had cast a left-of-center vote before the war. There was no hint of reservation about serving God and King as a chaplain in the struggle.

As the weeks of 1914 turned into the months of 1915, however, some of the illusions of his youth began to wear off. He marked his twenty-ninth birthday on August 20, 1915, in a two-day celebration with fellow officers.[1] The war began in earnest for Tillich in Champagne in northeastern France in October, 1915. Months of trench warfare followed.

His first experience with heavy fighting came on October 30–31 when the Germans assaulted the heights of Tahure. The objectives were not all achieved, and the losses were very heavy. The first days of November were dedicated to visiting the wounded and burying the dead. As Tillich dropped the sticky loam of the Champagne onto the coffins of friends in the officer corps, an inner grimness of spirit overcame him. The mass burials of the soldiers deepened his grief. After days of living through such trauma, he knew that a time would come when the numbness that shielded one from the horror of death would break.[2] Occasionally unable to preach, sometimes claiming that God himself was preaching the message in the slaughter, he did gather himself together to preach after the battle at Tahure. He drew upon Paul from 2 Corinthians 4:17–18.

> For this slight momentary affliction is preparing for us an eternal weight of glory beyond all comparison, because we look not to the things that are unseen; for the things that are seen are transient, but the things that are unseen are eternal.[3]

The preacher confessed his inability to speak of things human to his listeners. Only the godly word could be heard. If they, the weary veterans and the new replacements, concentrated on things visible they would see suffering and death. His dear war comrades could only despair of the present. Their only recourse rested in meditating on the things eternal. The blood-soaked ground of the Champagne held no comfort. But by turning to the invisible, comfort and meaning could be found. They could be faithful to themselves for the holy love of the homeland and for the pride of being German and for the bonds of community and for the magnificence of the great German fatherland. All these qualities were invisible, but they were true and worth more than comfort. That which is seen is temporary and passes away; only the unseen will endure. He told the soldiers that their heroism had eternity in it.

Then he turned to the question of the fallen comrades and meditated on the despair if death were the end. He comforted the troops with the promise of eternal life, again contrasting the meanness and coarseness of the visible with the beauty and eternity of the invisible. Addressing the new replacements whose shock at the carnage equalled Tillich's own, he asked them to look beyond the visible world of war. He feared that the visible reality would cause their hearts to shrink from the task. He called them to realize their brotherhood in arms and to see in every work a service to the great German fatherland, in every suffering the spirit of holy love, and in every death of simple sacrifice, eternal greatness.

In conclusion he called the new troops and old troops to bind themselves into one spirit of a new flaming enthusiasm, to remain strong and cheerful, and to achieve victory over the external enemy and the enemy within their own hearts. He urged them to concentrate on the invisible in spite of the visible because the invisible is eternal.

The sermon does not contain the notes of resignation and defeat that are found in his report on the months of November and December, 1915. The sermon attempts to use belief in an invisible realm of meaning to strengthen men for the visible task before which they quake. Despite claiming divine authority, certain aspects of the sermon, like imperial-German nationalism, do not seem in retrospect to have been eternal. It is the sermon of an army chaplain and of a chaplain whose world of meaning is crumbling. At the time of the sermon the world had not quite gone, but further suffering would overcome it. Many gods have been defeated in battle, and the secure god of bourgeois Germany and of Tillich's young adulthood was about to be defeated.

Gradually the significance of mass graves for troops and coffins for officers and of the church's blessing of the governmental blundering that led to the tragedy of World War I dawned upon him. He had entered the war without political consciousness; but gradually, as the war continued, his thinking became influenced by the socialist critique of the crumbling German society.

In May of 1916 the Seventh Division with its young chaplain went into the trenches of Verdun. Tillich's first weakening of nerves was followed by a brief respite from the trenches. His recovery permitted him a furlough during which he delivered a lecture at the University of Halle in his quest for a position there.[4]

The fighting continued and was interspersed with rest periods and some intellectual work. As a chaplain he demonstrated an empathy with men from all sections of German society and gained a reputation as a creative leader who risked himself in combat to tend the wounded.

In October of 1916 he collapsed in battle and was sent to the hospital. His own suffering merged into his consciousness of the dying of hundreds within his sight, millions in the war, and an epoch in European civilization. Gradually in the midst of death, the resurrection of Tillich began. He was becoming a new person.

In November he wrote that he was becoming thoroughly eschatological. He meditated and preached on the end. The world was in darkness and meaning was eschatological. The end came to dominate his mind, and he alternated between joy and despair.[5]

At thirty years of age he turned to new resources for strength. His speculation about a system of sciences led him out of the empirical. On leave he devoured art museums, and on post he turned to art books. Reading Nietzsche in the French forest, he found an affirmation of life that girded him for the remaining struggle and helped him to plan for his role in the future.[6]

Tillich was more fortunate than the twenty-year-old recruits. Erich Maria Remarque's *All Quiet on the Western Front* details how these younger men, without careers, without their own families, and alienated from their parents, went to pieces under the pounding of bombardment. Tillich had his doctorate; he had a wife; he had a promise of a future; he had religious faith and philosophy. Yet, death dominated him; there was no empirical hope. His philosophy and faith were idealist. In the French woods surrounded by death, he found in Friedrich Nietzsche's *Thus Spake Zarathustra* an exultation of life that revived him. Later Nietzsche's *The Will to Power* became important in his own writing on power. Nietzsche's glimpse of life as an emergence of the will to power had its origins in his own service in the Franco-Prussian War of 1870. Here in 1916 it encouraged Tillich to see the possibilities of life being born anew out of the severing of life that was the Western Front. The life emerging for

Tillich was a resurrected life, but also one that was as thoroughly Dionysiac as it was Christian. Much later he would say of Nietzsche: "Although his life was full of misery, in opposition to this he affirmed it infinitely."[7] Something of this affirmation Tillich wrested from Nietzsche in the midst of slaughter. Tillich never accepted all of Nietzsche's critique of Christianity, his normlessness, his notion of the eternal return, or his superior-man concept, but elements of Nietzsche's philosophy of life and ontology of the will remain in Tillich's thought.

Death of the Bourgeois God

The god of king and fatherland died in the trenches of France. Tillich speculated in a letter to Maria Klein in December, 1917, that justification by faith could lead to the paradox of faith without God.[8] Philosophically the old god was dead even if homiletically his death was not announced in sermons to the troops. The argument that one could be faithful while doubting or denying the existence of God was to continue as a recurring theme of Tillich's philosophy of religion. Faith as the state of being ultimately concerned did not, after the crisis of life in the midst of death at the French front, have to imply traditional Christian affirmations about God.[9] The god of king and fatherland had also been the god of his father. With the death of this god, the repressions of a patriarchal political, social, and familial order were thrown off, and the Dionysian element of Nietzsche—seeking life in affirmative actions beyond bourgeois morality —was accepted and lived.

A religious crisis in one of the kaiser's chaplains did not hinder the war effort. The attacking through the mud of northeastern France continued with Tillich suffering from hunger, fear, and shock. As attack, retreat, and counterattack continued over the same earth day after day with the mounting of casualties, the chaplain became increasingly distraught by the role of the religious-ideological establishment in sending these millions to their premature, terrible deaths.

Slowly those at the front came to realize that the Allies had more fresh men, more food, more shells, and more new equipment. Tillich deepened his study in philosophy when he could and sought succor in art, which his Lutheran heritage had not stressed. In April, 1918, he collapsed once more. From the hospital he attempted to get ecclesiastical authorities to secure his release from the army.[10] He felt that his resources were used up and that he could be of no more use to the war effort. He feared for his sanity—he had seen so many lose their minds—but his attempt to win release was thwarted. He was returned to his unit.

A letter written in May reflects a change of mood, expressing the joy of the victor as German forces, and his division in particular, enjoyed success near the Marne. Tillich was awarded the Iron Cross by the commander of the division. In August he was assigned to Berlin, and there he remained through the end of the war. He was spared the final defeats in France, but soon he was to witness the return of the defeated armies and revolution in Berlin.

At the front Tillich had known hunger, fear, exhaustion, the death of comrades, and mental breakdown. He doubted his own recovery. He had learned the cunning tactics of those who survive at the front. He had experienced the banal excesses of troops on leave. He had known the comfort of philosophy and the failure of traditional religion. The idealist philosopher of the nineteenth century had been thrown into the existence of the twentieth century. His own life had been exposed in a way that later he would use Freud to understand. Nietzsche had helped him live in the hell of Verdun. Now, in Berlin, Marx gave him insights with which to understand the war politically, and in the last months of 1918, the disillusioned soldier turned into a radical. This encounter with Marx was to continue in a life-long dialogue.

Continuity in Tillich's life is more impressive than change, however. The war was not, as Wilhelm and Marion Pauck have asserted, best understood as a turning point; rather, it is a bridge. His suffering challenged his philosophical idealism and his Lutheran faith, but they were not surrendered. At the beginning of the war, he was a young doctor of philosophy and a pastor; at the end of the war, he was a war chaplain working on philosophic problems. The war is the connection in experience between Tillich the essentialist and Tillich the existentialist, and both aspects must be seen to comprehend his ethical political philosophy, which is a synthesis of nineteenth and twentieth century thought and experience. The nineteenth century had given him strengths that the war, as long as it permitted him to survive in body and mind, could not erase.

IV.
Radical in Berlin

Tillich's final months as a chaplain to the kaiser's army were spent in revolutionary Berlin. During the time he was posted at the base of Spandau in the capital—August 1, 1918, to the end of his service in December—the army fell apart and the kaiser was forced to abdicate. On November 9 a long series of strikes, rallies, mutinies, and political maneuverings culminated in a bloodless victory for the forces demanding a republic. In the political confusion that followed, the reluctant Social Democrats assumed power and, with the help of the old bureaucracy and military establishment, managed to govern and withstand assaults from the right and the left.

Tillich's political consciousness was developing during these turbulent months. It emerged in the church-state controversy, and the available evidence places him to the left of the Social Democrats and reveals him to be far more radical than the progressive elements of the Evangelical church. Ernst Troeltsch and Max Weber, for example, were leaders in the Democratic party, which was to the right of the Social Democrats (SDP). Tillich's father and most of the leadership of the church had been staunch monarchists and only reluctantly supported the republic while resisting the separation of the church and state, which the provisional government moved immediately to accomplish. The church people were fundamentally shaken at the action, and their protests overwhelmed the government's initiative.

The attempt was ultimately defeated, and the church-state alliance remained almost as secure as it had been under the kaiser. There were, however, several groups of church people who supported the separation and saw it as an opportunity to renew the church.

New Church

Tillich signed a statement by one of the minor groups supporting the separation of church and state.[1] The announcement by the New Church Alliance was made in December, only a few days after Wilhelm formally surrendered his throne. Tillich was leaving the army at the time and accepting a position in the church and as a junior faculty member at the University of Berlin. Cosignatories with Dr. Paul Tillich, *Privatdozent,* were three other pastors, an author, and two women. Dr. Paul Aner organized the group to which Tillich committed his first recorded radical political action.

The announcement, which called for conventions to meet throughout the country and form a new basis for the church of the evolving future, recognized that the old church had become hated and that revolutionary public opinion was calling for the separation of church and state. This separation was a threat to the Evangelical church. Because a church was needed to maintain religious power, to encourage religious life, and to implement a religious culture, however, free people were called upon to implement an alliance for a new church. The program of the alliance was summarized under four points.

The first thesis argued that the power of the church had been squandered in internal, dogmatic bickering. The new church was to remain neutral on questions that had previously divided the church, seeking instead to renew religious motifs in the general culture. The second point indicated that, while the previous church had been conservative in political outlook, the new church supported the new republic and a farsighted socialism. The personal worth of each citizen in the community was affirmed over against the capitalist egoism that had characterized the previous order. Third, the new church would be aligned with the international peace movement and would reject the militarism and nationalism that had characterized the old church. A system of international justice was advocated to replace the old way of power politics. The final point of the announcement was an attack upon the old hierarchical organization of the church. A form of parliamentary control was planned to govern the church. The clergy would find new freedom in their professional groups, which would replace the old bureaucracy. The right of women to vote in the new church was announced, and the announcement itself was addressed to all Evangelical men *and women* in Germany.

Tillich did not participate actively in the New Church Alliance for very long; it merged within a year with a league of religious socialists. But this document remains his first recorded political statement. He continued to emphasize concern for the renewal of the religious aspects of culture and the need to free the church from conservative control, though the thrust toward pacifism is not characteristic of the rest of his work.

The revolution was not to go forward in the church. After much struggle the church retained its privileges and its antipathy toward socialism. Symbolic of the superficiality of change in the church is the letter appointing Tillich to a post as a city pastor in 1918.[2] Written on December 12, it is on the letterhead stationery of the *Konigliches Konsistorium der Provinz Brandenburg* (Royal Consistory of the Province of Brandenburg). *Konigliches* has been crossed out and the word *Evangelisches* (Evangelical) typed in to signify the reformed nature of the church. The king was gone, but the spirit of the imperial church remained.

Christian Socialism

On May 16, 1919, the President of the Consistory D. Steinhauser wrote to Tillich informing him that the newspaper *Zehlendorfer Anzeiger* had reported that he had spoken at a rally of the Independent Social Democrats on the theme of Christian socialism.[3] The president requested a report on the matter.

The Independent Social Democrats were the most radical of the socialists. Though the Communist party of Germany, led by Luxemburg and Liebknecht, had attracted the more extreme members of the Independents in December, 1918, those who remained were still to the left of the Social Democrats and were outside the power structure. They and the Communists were repressed by the military. On January 15, 1919, Liebknecht and Luxemburg were murdered, and rioting in Berlin was crushed by the military. In March twelve hundred workers were killed in the capital, and on May 1 the Soviet Republic of Munich was stamped out in blood and terror. The anti-Bolshevik fear was rampant, and when Tillich addressed the rally, the middle class was desperately trying to restore the situation as it had been before the revolution.

Tillich had been lecturing on "Christianity and the Social Problems of the Present" at the University of Berlin, and his appearance at the Independent Social Democratic rally revealed the commitments of the teacher. Though he never joined the Independent party, he voted with them in these early days as the only democratic party committed to fundamental change. During the week of the rally, the Independents were meeting throughout Berlin demanding that Germany sign the Versailles Treaty and leave the results to the coming world revolution.[4] The other parties were opposed to the signing, and by May the political turmoil in both church and state was tremendous.

Richard Wegener, a pastor to youth in Berlin, was probably the leader in the rally incident. He, too, was called to answer for his conduct, and he was the joint author with Tillich of their report to the Brandenburg Consistory.[5] "Dox" Wegener was one of Tillich's closest friends. He had become romantically involved with Tillich's wife, and he fathered Grethi's child to whom Tillich gave his name before he and Grethi were divorced. Nevertheless, Tillich and Wegener maintained their friendship, even to the extent of carousing together on the evening of Tillich's second marriage. The correspondence between them into their old age reveals their continued affection and admiration for each other. Eventually Wegener would resign from the ministry because of his socialism and enter government service at the invitation of Ernst Troeltsch, under secretary of state in the Ministry of Education in the republic.

Wegener and Tillich responded to Steinhauser by outlining the content of their speeches and stating their position on Christian socialism. Later their report was published in a revised form under the title of "Socialism as a Question of the Church."

The report was divided into sections on Christianity and society, socialism and Christianity, and the church's task regarding socialism. The authors first confessed the independence of the encounter with God and its transcendence of particular social conditions, affirming that religion has an inward personal character beyond any particular economic or social form. However, as Christianity carries with it the drive to shape life, they argued, it cannot be regarded as purely personal or inward, for it is inevitably involved in society. It has, historically, connected itself with the various social orders under which it has lived. Christianity is more inclined toward some orders than others; love has social consequences. The report stated a belief that the egoist competition of capitalism resulting in militarism is in opposition to Christianity. Furthermore, the authors argued that socialism has greater affinity with Christianity than capitalism. Christianity is challenged to decide whether to move into the emerging social order or to remain in a conservative defense of the old order. The second part of the short paper argued that socialism has no essential fight with religion or Christianity. The atheism of some socialist leaders has been coincidental and unnecessary, they claimed. Socialism needs religion. Socialism may be against clerical privileges and state-bestowed benefits for the church, but when it understands itself, socialism is not irreligious. In the third part of the report, Tillich and Wegener argued that the church should adopt a positive attitude toward socialism. They distinguished their concerns from the movement to reform the church to attract the working classes. Socialism, they said, is a new ethical ideal emerging from the experience of the working class, and it expresses the proper social ethic of the church.

Steinhauser's reaction to their report was negative, and he ordered them not to speak at any more rallies.[6] He gave as reasons the dislike of such expressions by church people and the danger of amalgamation of religion and politics.

During 1919 Tillich met once a week with a group of young intellectuals, most of whom were theologians, to discuss the relationship of the church to socialism. The group had been formed by a community service house known as *Soziale Arbeitsgemeinschaft*. Günther Dehn's report on the group indicates that on one occasion Dehn discussed Hermann Kutter and Leonhard Ragaz's essays, Karl Mennicke talked on his theories of a people's church *(Volkskirche)*, and Tillich outlined Ragaz's theology.[7] This reference establishes a connection between Tillich and the prominent Swiss religious socialist for whom the roots of religious socialism reached back to the work of Christoph Blumhardt (1842–1919) in Württemberg. Ragaz was the inspiration for Karl Barth's religious socialism, while Tillich's owed more to events and to Karl Marx.

Ernst Troeltsch came once to the group. His work in philosophy of history and in ethics had a profound effect upon Tillich, but Troeltsch's politics were more moderate and, consequently, had little influence upon Tillich's religious socialism. The group evolved, and Tillich and Mennicke lost interest in it. They were looking for a way to address the foundational questions of religion and socialism more directly.

In his 1919 review of *Revolution and the Church,* Tillich demanded that thinking go beyond mere reform.[8] He charged that the liberal reformist views of Troeltsch, Martin Rode, and Rudolf Otto, contributors to the volume, were not adequate to deal with the social crisis that called for a reformulation of both religion and socialism. During this time the Evangelical Social Congress also addressed social problems. However, it refused to make a socialist commitment, and Tillich found it unable to transcend its capitalist origins.[9]

Tillich's search for an answer adequate to both his religious faith and his radical socialism led him in 1920 into a group that became known as the Kairos Circle.[10] He remained a leader of this group until he left Berlin in 1924. Through this period of extreme political confusion with attempted putsches and assassinations, including that of the foreign minister Walter Rathenau, this circle of intellectuals focused their attention upon the following areas: the relationship of the eternal to the historical, Marxism, solidarity with the proletariat, and the nature of the fulfillment of socialist society. Mennicke edited the group's journal, *Blätter für religiösen Sozialismus* (1920–1927), and wrote most of the essays. Tillich contributed many essays to the journal as did the other members of the circle, Eduard Heimann, Adolf Löwe, Alexander Rüstow, and Arnold Wolfers. The group was religious in inspiration—about half Protestant and half Jewish.

Heimann, an economist, and Löwe, a civil servant and an economist, provided Tillich with his knowledge of economics, and Wolfers deepened his acquaintance with political theory. While they were in Berlin, Mnnicke, Rüstow, and Wolfers were connected with the *Deutsche Hochschule für Politik,* and through them Tillich kept in touch with developments in social criticism in a manner similar to the role to be played by the Institute for Social Research in Frankfurt in the 1930s.

Tillich's articulation of his kairos philosophy owed much to discussions within the circle. Examination of the idea of kairos reveals Tillich's passionate search for a way to explicate the relationship of the eternal to the temporal, the significant to the passing, and activism to social philosophy.

V.
Kairos and Religious Socialism

The years from 1919 to 1924 were the turbulent, chaotic, heady years of the Weimar Republic, for by 1925 some semblance of stability was achieved. Tillich lived in Berlin until the spring of 1924, and while sympathetic to the radical Independents at whose rally he had spoken, his primary political education was in the discussion group of socialist intellectuals that took the name of the Kairos Circle. Tillich's 1922 essay, "Kairos," explicates the centrality of this concept to the group's philosophy of history. His essay of 1923, *"Grundlinien des religiösen Sozialismus,"* expresses the outlines of his political philosophy at that time. Not all members of the Kairos Circle would accept totally the thought of these essays, but they are representative of Tillich's contributions to the group.

His concepts of kairos and religious socialism were shaped by the political life that affected all who lived in Berlin. The 1919 national elections witnessed the overwhelming victory of the Social Democrats. They polled 11.5 million votes. Their nearest rival was the Catholic Center party with almost 6 million votes, and the Liberal Democrats polled approximately 5.5 million. The government was formed from these three parties, and Philipp Scheidemann presided over the coalition cabinet. Friedrich Ebert, the president, promised to rule for all Germans while not forsaking his working-class origins and his socialist principles. The National Constitutional Assembly met in Weimar partially because of the continuing disorder in Berlin. It was becoming clear that the Independents and the Communists would not share in the power and that the socialist measures of the new Weimar coalition would be moderate.

Democracy was assailed by both the extreme right and the extreme left. The crippling pressures, however, came from the victorious allies who forced the German government to accept the Versailles Peace Treaty. The coalition broke over the acceptance of the new borders, the loss of colonies, the economic reparations, and the insults to the German nation. A new government was formed, but in accepting the treaty, the Social Democrats were damned from all sides in Germany. The bold new experiment in democracy was being strangled by the victorious democratic nations which seemed unaware that the empire they had opposed in the war had been transformed into a struggling democracy. As history would teach us, the Treaty of Versailles officially ending the war also lost the peace. The theory spread that a proud Germany had not lost the war on the battlefield but by domestic betrayal. Those who were forced to support the treaty, however reluctantly, were seen as the traitors.

The Constitution was promulgated in August of 1919, and in September the government moved to Berlin. The Weimar Constitution was a mixture of socialist and liberal principles reflecting the alliance of Social Democrats, Democrats, and Center interests. It was written in the midst of civil disorder, even civil war, and immense powers for the protection of social order were given to the president. The Independents and Nationalists opposed the Constitution, and the hatred between the Independents and Social Democrats reached a new intensity in January, 1920, when rioting before the Reichstag resulted in forty-two people being killed by troops. The Social Democrats' hold on the workers weakened, and hostility to the government from the left deepened.

Political life in Germany stumbled from one crisis into another. Resisting Allied demands for the reduction of the army, rightist leaders moved against the government. A brigade occupied Berlin, and the government fled. Wolfgang Kapp was installed as head of a revolutionary government. The Social Democrats' appeal for a general strike was honored by the unions, however, and German industry stopped. The ineptness of the conspirators, the resistance to the putsch by the proletariat, and the steadfast unity of the constitutional government caused the revolutionaries to surrender their positions.

In the Ruhr, utopian socialists launched a Red Army counterattack that left them in control of several key industrial cities. The French retaliated by occupying Frankfurt on April 6, 1920. The newly formed Hermann Mueller government, again a coalition of Center, Democrat, and Social Democrat, was able to secure the withdrawal of France in the middle of May. This social disorder was accompanied by the decline in the value of the currency and widespread lawlessness, which shook the authority of the government.

The elections of 1920 produced a sharp decline in the voting strength of both the Democrats and the Social Democrats. The center was weakened, while both rightist parties and leftist Independents scored substantial gains. The Independents attracted 4,895,317 votes, only slightly behind the Social Democrats' 5,614,456. These elections revealed the trends that were to dominate the Weimar Republic: the eroding of the center and the rise of the extreme parties.

The refusal of the Independents to join a moderate government with the Social Democrats permitted a new coalition to emerge, and the SPD was out of power in 1920 only two years after the formation of the new government. The process of socialization of the economy was set back further.

The growth of fighting groups on both sides of the political spectrum increased the instability of society. Walter Rathenau, the liberal Jewish foreign minister, was assassinated by right-wing nationalists on June 24, 1922. "Organization C," the refuge of supporters of the Kapp putsch, was responsible. The murderers were caught, but as usual, the government was unable to enforce stiff penalties against conspirators from the right.

Throughout 1923 strikes and moves for the secession of areas of the Ruhr and Bavaria kept Germany in turmoil. The Hitler-Ludendorf attempted putsch in 1923 in Munich was suppressed, and the importance of Hitler was unappreciated. In the elections of December, 1924, the Nazis were so soundly defeated that they appeared to be of no political significance.

Kairos

The foundations of the world seemed to be shaking. The death throes of the old empire prevented the emergence of a new order, which was divided among bourgeois, fascist, and radical groups. The political issue involved in the concept of Tillich's Kairos Circle was: How can we affirm action for decisive change without surrendering to the enthusiasms of the activists? Or, put in terms of Marxist groups: How can we mediate between the determinists and the romantic activists? Experience taught that action, or praxis, was vital to social change, but action had to be in accord with the objective social conditions. In religious terms the question in the Kairos Circle was: How does the eternal relate to the temporal? To combine the religious and the political questions was to ask: When are moments of historical action eternally significant?

Tillich's essay "Kairos" is a call to a consciousness of history that is grounded in the "depth of the unconditional."[1] The unconditional is expressed as a quality of experience that is absolute or ultimate. It is captured in the first commandment, "Thou shalt love the Lord thy God with *all* thy heart. . . ." As a philosophy of history, it is set against all forms of understanding history that deny it meaning.

The concept of kairos has its origins in the New Testament where it means "right time" as opposed to chronos, or "formal time." The demands and opportunities of each time vary. The moments of absolute demand are the moments of kairos.[2] The idea that particular times are filled with significance is contrasted both to Eastern mystical tendencies, which would deny the significance of history, and to Western mechanistic thinking, which would obscure the significance of history.

The danger of the crisis theology of Karl Barth was that the significance of the present might be eclipsed. Barth was correct to relativize all historical creations. There is no absolute church or absolute state. But Tillich insists that when an old order is passing and a new order is emerging, the new order is *en kairo*. The new order is subject to judgment and change, but its coming is the content of history. The absolute comes in the new creation and in the judgment of the old. For Tillich, obviously, the new socialist order was in the right time in the early Weimar Republic.

The philosophy of history represented by kairos is close to dialectical interpretations of history, but in the kairos interpretation, there is no final stage. The age of the spirit (Joachim) and the classless society (Marx) are not to be thought of as final stages; they, too, are subject to criticism and transformation. The kairos interpretation tries to retain the idea of classical history, in which each moment is significant, and also the conviction of progress, which affirms the appearance of the new in history.

Tillich settles for a paradox. In the moment of kairos the absolute is expressed; yet, it is not an absolute. Judgment and further transformation await every realization. The proper response in such a situation is to refrain from trying to capture the absolute; rather, one should surrender to it. Christ, as the one who surrenders the self, is clearly the norm for life in moments of kairos. As Christ reveals the individual surrendering to the universal, so in moments of personal kairos or social kairos the particular is to be surrendered to the universal. Clearly, Tillich is using his Christology as a formulation for a philosophy of history, but for him the secular images of "the third epoch of world history" or the "Kingdom of God" can express the same reality.[3]

In the early twenties a time of kairos was confronting the Western world. Religious socialism was the theological interpretation of socialism in light of the kairos philosophy. In 1922 the rudimentary ideas that were to be expressed in *The Religious Situation* of 1926 and *The Socialist Decision* of 1933 were present. The task of religious socialism was the theoretical task of reminding socialism of its roots in the unconditional. Religious socialism had to attempt to free socialism from its bourgeois loyalties. Tillich rejected the attempts to unite socialism with the churches, for the alliance would only strengthen them; whereas, both needed to be thoroughly criticized and transformed.

In 1951 he returned to Berlin and lectured at the *Deutsche Hochschule für Politik* with which many of the original members of the Kairos Circle had been associated. His lectures were on utopia, but he returned to the doctrine of the kairos. He expressed the concept as a way of saying both yes and no at the moment of decision. Yes must be said to the absolute demand for action. No, however, must be said to the demand for an absolute solution, which would be idolatrous. New orders can be born and are in history; but they, too, will be transformed. Fulfillment, he said, is found in the vertical dimension of history; on the horizontal level, fulfillment is always fragmentary.[4] Looking back on history since the end of World War I, he concluded that the interwar reflections on kairos were correct.

In the final part of *Systematic Theology* Tillich also returned to the theme of kairos and acknowledged the emergence of the term in the context of religious socialism.[5] In part the kairos that was expected had been fulfilled, in part it had not arrived, and in part it was betrayed by the Nazis. "Awareness of a *kairos* is a matter of vision."[6] It is the surrendering to the spirit that is doing something new. It is a full affirmation of what is happening beyond calculation and analysis. Such affirmation is, of course, subject to error. Against theologians and philosophers who supported the Nazis, Tillich argued that the "Cross of Christ was and is the absolute criterion."[7] Moments of kairos are rare, and because Tillich regarded the interwar period as such a time, he also thought that a future kairos for Western civilization was postponed until the rather distant future. The discussion of kairos in *Systematic Theology* of 1963 is essentially the same as his discussion of kairos in the 1922 essay and is evidence of the fundamental continuity in his thought.

Religious Socialism

In 1923 he published in the journal of the Kairos Circle the lengthy essay, "Basic Principles of Religious Socialism."[8] The essay incorporates work from *The System of the Sciences,* published in the same year, and which he had been working on since his days on the Western Front. Some of the concepts of the essay are found, in more developed form, in both "Philosophy of Religion," published in 1925, and in *The Socialist Decision* of 1933.

Religious socialism as a movement is identified with neither a church nor a political party. The movement is a community of those who are grasped by the kairos of a new time and who hope that the

emerging order can be both religious and socialist. Religious socialists, while joining in the socialist political struggles, do not bless
them with religious sanction. The tactics of the socialist parties, they
believe, do not express the fullness of the socialist idea.[9]

Religious socialism, according to Tillich, is an attempt to reunite
the sacramental basis of society with historical critical consciousness.
In religion such a union would be represented by a synthesis of
Catholic substance and Protestant critique. Socially, the union is a
meaningful society utilizing modern techniques.

The goal of religious socialism is nothing less than theonomy,
meaning the sovereignty of God or "God is all in all." Tillich
distinguishes theonomy from both worldly and other-worldly utopianism.[10] It preserves the affirmation of religion to socialism as well
as the religious reservations about socialism. Similarly, the religion
that contains self-critical elements is most open to what the Spirit is
doing in society. Expressed in terms of social ethics, theonomy is the
right and the just. Concretely, it operates in opposition to demonic
distortions of humanity's life.

In the area of economics, Tillich argues that the modern, rational
economy denies personality as fully as did feudalism. He looks for
a restoration of an eros relationship between person and thing. His
meaning is not clear, but his intention seems close to that of the
young Marx, the overcoming of the person's alienation from product. There is explicit rejection of the criticism of machines; rather,
the need is to find a new scheme of meaning that will allow people
to participate significantly in a "*mythos* of technology."[11] The pattern
is a familiar one for Tillich, the critique of modern autonomous
society and the seeking of a new basis for it.

The rational, capitalist society is organized demonically in that its
foundation is the war of all against all in competition. The class
struggle reveals the disharmony underlying the capitalist order. The
reduction of all relationships of power and eros to economic terms
denies the individual his subjective rights and leaves only objective,
dependent relationships. In the new society envisaged by Tillich,
there is a return to some models associated with feudal society, but,
of course, without power to pass on privilege to descendants or to
hold to possession after the action's significance for the whole com-

munity has passed. He mentions the idea of "fief" whereby one has disposition of goods in relationship to the needs of the community. The society has a certain hierarchy of function as determined by the needs of the whole. Ideas of property through fief and the functional use of property replace both state ownership and private ownership in his understanding of religious socialism.[12]

Presently, the state is the defender of justice. Justice is upheld by power. Religious socialism rejects various forms of anarchism and accepts the present reality of the state while combating nationalism, particularly in its idolatrous forms. As Tillich hopes for an aristocracy to emerge to lead the struggle for a theonomous society, so in international affairs he hopes "the strongest bearers of the theonomous idea of humanity should constitute the leadership of nations."[13] There is a religious reservation about force—Tolstoy symbolizes such a reservation—but religious socialism cannot abandon the power that will sustain justice.

The particular expressions of the theonomous society were, for Tillich, provisional. Meanwhile, religious socialists were to struggle to overthrow the demonic in education, state, and culture while awaiting the breakthrough to the new society.[14]

Tillich's writing on religious socialism in the turmoil of Berlin expressed the spirit of utopianism more than it did political realism. His awareness of the class struggle kept him from endorsing the Social Democratic party, but he could not give himself enthusiastically to the Independents either. The idea of kairos would remain central to his philosophy of society, but later reflection on the class struggle and continuing discussion with social philosophers would produce in Dresden and Frankfurt a more immanent religious socialism and a more realistic political outlook.

VI.
Faithful Realism

The election of Field Marshal Paul von Hindenburg to the presidency in April, 1925, meant the victory of the counterrevolution. In 1926 Germany was admitted to the League of Nations and in 1928 signed the Kellogg-Briand Pact outlawing war. General prosperity was restored. After the troubled years of 1919–1924, the period from 1925 to 1928 could be viewed as a return to normalcy. By 1928 when the Social Democrats returned to power, their revolutionary fervor had waned.

Tillich joined the Social Democratic party in 1929. His philosophy was still to the left of the party, but he realized that one could not stay aloof from commitment. The SPD was the only option for a democratic socialist, and he took it. The years from 1925 to 1929 were years of personal success for Tillich. In 1925 he moved from Berlin to Marburg, and then to the University of Dresden. While at Dresden he also taught theology at the University of Leipzig. In 1929 he succeeded Max Scheler as professor of philosophy at the University of Frankfurt. The evolution of his political thought during these years is seen in his book criticizing bourgeois society and in his essays on "faithful realism," Augustine's political theory, the demonic, and the class struggle.

The Religious Situation

Adolf Hitler's *Mein Kampf* and Paul Tillich's *Die religiöse Lage der Gegenwart (The Religious Situation)*, both completed in 1926, attacked the meaningless of the society from which they came. Tillich's socialism was, of course, anathema to Hitler, and Hitler's anti-Semitism was antithetical to all Tillich represented.

Tillich's book is filled with historically detailed evaluations of many movements in Germany, including science, metaphysics, art, politics, ethics, and religion. The major sources of his argument are the perspectives of his religious socialist circles and the work of Max Weber and Ernst Troeltsch. Weber and Troeltsch provide the major categories of interpretation.

The influence of Weber's classic study, *The Protestant Ethic and the Spirit of Capitalism,* is evident in the central conception of the book.[1] Tillich's use of "the spirit of capitalist society" seems to be an idea dependent on Weber's use of the same term. In both authors it is an attempt to capture in an expression the characteristic drive of Western humanity. Tillich calls it a "symbol,"[2] but it serves the same function as Weber's "ideal type." Tillich, more than Weber, is interested in conquering that attitude of "the capitalist spirit"; his socialism is more consistent and thoroughgoing than Weber's reformist liberal socialism, just as his religious philosophy is deeper and more profound than Weber's agnosticism.

The spirit of capitalist society is the dominance of the world by a particular form of economic activity, which is committed to a view of humanity as competing, finite, consuming, producing units. It is the reduction of human life to mechanical analysis and the utilization of science and technology to promote an economic system committed to the exclusion of the infinite. The capitalist spirit is the breaking of attitudes of awe toward the material world and the turning of human life toward the endless pursuit of finite things. Tillich opposes the "self-sufficient finitude" that he sees as the driving force of capitalist society, and he challenges it in terms of response to the unconditional.

The influence of Troeltsch in this book is seen in the general position that the existing churches have no adequate social response to the twentieth century.[3] Tillich's division of the churches into mysticism, sects, and churches when he analyzes the churches' response to the spirit of capitalism is taken from Troeltsch. Tillich also agrees with Troeltsch about the relative ineffectiveness of existing religious socialism, but then he attempts a new synthesis of religion and socialism.

To understand the religious situation in his culture, Tillich begins with a study of the broader culture. Leadership in the twentieth century had passed out of the hands of ecclesiastical groups. The churches followed cultural trends. The overwhelming trend in the culture was one in metaphysics, science, art, politics, and ethics that settled for finitude and remained only slightly troubled by references to the infinite. Capitalist society, Tillich assumes, is committed to excluding the eternal from life.[4] Consequently, the study of the religious situation demands an understanding of the economic dominance of the culture that results in the exclusion of the symbols of eternity. Forces of protest against the competitive self-sufficiency of a bourgeois economy buttressed by technology, science, and liberal economics arose at the end of the nineteenth century. Nietzsche, Strindberg, and van Gogh represented the protest, and their destruction symbolized the difficulty of the struggle.

In his reflection on the present, *Gegenwart,* Tillich reflects on the past out of which the present had come, the future with which it is in tension, and the eternal, or unconditioned, meaning of the present. The eternal is perceived by "faith in the unconditioned meaning of life."[5] If one begins the inquiry from the side of the eternal rather than from the human side, then one must pursue the eternal in all human cultural forms. Conversely, the inquiry from the side of humanity would begin with the religious forms. Tillich takes the former option, and only after inquiring into the spiritual expression of important cultural forms does he look at the spiritual expression of the particular religious forms.

Tillich argues for a "faithful realism" as a perspective for metaphysics, politics, art, and ethics. He unites "faithful" (gläubiger) as a response of faith to the unconditioned, with "realism" (realismus) as the steadfast commitment to see particulars. H. Richard Niebuhr has suggested that to understand the term one should first think of realism as it is used in art or history.[6] Though focus on particulars is needed, it does not reveal the full meaning. In history Tillich wants to unite the study of a particular epoch with an inquiry into its eternal meaning. Neither time nor eternity is to be denied.

In the protests against the cultural liberalism of Judaism, Catholicism, and Protestantism, he affirms the prophetic critique of Karl Barth in denying that any finite expression of a culture can capture the divine. He also affirms the mysticism of his colleague at Marburg Rudolph Otto. Tillich seeks for a way to unite the best of Protestant criticism with the best of the religious substance of mysticism. In this 1926 work he is still affirming the necessity of uniting the critical consciousness of ethical-prophetic religion with mysticism as he had in his second dissertation on Schelling. The union of the priestly and the prophetic he called faithful realism.

In 1927 and 1928 he returned to the theme of faithful realism in essays.[7] The second of these essays is breathtaking in scope and reveals Tillich at his creative best.[8] Expressionism and Postexpressionism in art exhibited a rebellion against naturalism and idealism. The paintings witnessed to the depths of reality by breaking natural forms and using color to express "divine and demonic ecstasies."[9] Tillich finds this same attitude of faithful realism in the fight against mystical realism and technical realism in philosophies of history. Faithful realism, he explains, means an analysis of the present historical situation in light of the eternal.

In both personal and social relations, faithful realism attempts to unite scientific objectivity with passion for the purpose of transformation. Romanticism tries to escape to a realm that never was. Utopianism tries to escape to a realm that never will be. *Realpolitik* only manipulates the present without regard to the depths of the present. Faithful realism knows that the unconditional, which is the depth of the human historical situation, cannot be grasped intellectually.

Here the evocation of Schelling is present; the *Unvordenkliche* is "the ground and abyss of everything that is."[10] The gap between humanity and God remains. Yet, the historical situation is interpreted by faithful realism as that which points in the direction of the unconditional. Tillich compares it to the situation in a thunderstorm:

the lightning illuminates all and then leaves it again in darkness. So in faith God grasps humanity, humanity responds in ecstasy, and the darkness is never again the same after the light. Mindful of the dangers of mysticism and ecstasy, Tillich nonetheless reveals in this essay his preference for these modes and the need to combine them with the most rigorous scholarship. The historical situation cannot be abandoned, or God is banned to a supernatural realm. However, the historical situation cannot be interpreted only in terms of the present, or faith is denied.

Augustine

In this period Tillich affirmed Augustine as his *Führer* (leader). Augustine acknowledged God as *"das unbedingte Sein"* (unconditional being) and related God's work to man's fallen state.[11] Augustine saw clearly that the state as the expression of communal-societal interests was under demonic control; yet, he saw also that God used even the demonic powers of the state to resist evil. Christians could not abandon the state, but neither should they be deceived about it. The state pursues its own peace, but on the basis of presuppositions with which it will never reach peace. Facing imperialism and capitalism, Tillich's society faced a question similar to that confronted by Augustine and early Christianity. Augustine's criticism of the state while refusing to abandon it was the answer for Tillich, who, as Augustine, had to reach into the depths of the meaning of history to ground his politics.

In 1925 when this essay on Augustine was published, Reinhold Niebuhr was still a young pastor in Detroit. Both in their own ways were working toward a theological partnership in which the social thought of Augustine would play a large role. Events in Europe had driven both to inquire after alternative theologies to their inheritance. Niebuhr, as the younger man, had not reached Augustine yet, but he would in the 1930s. The many congruencies of their political thought would emerge in the thirties and forties.

The Demonic

It is evident that part of Tillich's attraction to Augustine's social thought is Augustine's use of the concept of the "demonic" in political thought. Along with faithful realism and kairos, the concept of the demonic became a central term of Tillich's political philosophy.

Tillich's social realism was more often characteristic of conservative politics than of either liberal or radical politics. In his political writing and speeches, he labored to convince his radical friends and allies that they should adopt a more realistic and less optimistic attitude. The realist side of his political "faithful realism" emphasized all the forces that resisted the struggle for a more just community. The emphasis on these forces was partially derived from empirical observation, but more fundamentally came from his total philosophy and its inclusion of the concept of the demonic.

Like several other important Tillichian concepts, demonic was originally expressed in the context of the interwar political struggle and has its roots in classical German philosophy. The 1926 essay *"Das Dämonishe, ein Beitrag zur Sinndeutung der Geschichte"* unites the philosophical roots of the concept and its political meaning in Tillich's best systematic exposition of the frequently used concept.[12]

In this essay he portrays capitalism and nationalism as the major demonic movements of his time. These ideational-structural forces are demonic because they unite elements of meaning and meaningless. Both capitalism and nationalism express the vitality of creative life that produces meaningful forms of existence, but both also contain the drive to destroy form and to deprive people of their essential humanity. In the interwar period, the demon of nationalism was subject to capitalism, producing immense power and threatening the destruction of European civilization. Both capitalism and nationalism generated claims for the control of life, and the claims of the nation in particular bordered on the sacred. Tillich argues that these forces are not demonic simply because he disapproves of them or because they are harmful; they are demonic because they so completely combine the creative and the destructive. In opposing the demonic, he cautions, there is no guarantee of success, however. Total resistance to the demonic is required, but the only certainty for religious faith is that the demonic will be vanquished ultimately; here in the period of the penultimate it may be supreme.

The conception in the political synthesis of the creative and the destructive becoming almost invincible has its roots in Tillich's ontology. "Demonry is the form-destroying eruption of the creative basis of things."[13] There is in Tillich's ontology no "independent eruption of the 'abyss'."[14] That is, form is not destroyed independent of form, for there is a unity of the form-creating and form-destroying capacities of life in the inexhaustibility of being. Everything that comes into being takes on a form; loss of the form means destruction. But in everything is also the tendency to realize in itself all being, the tendency in life to break out of a being's own form to realize infinity. Here, the prideful assertion of one's being is taken as exemplary of this tendency in being.

The inexhaustibility of Tillich's concept of being is not interpreted in static terms, but is seen as a "consuming fire." Being itself is not passive but active, uniting form-creation and form-destruction in the divine life. In the discussion of the demonic, the intuitive-mystical character of Tillich's thought is obvious. The debt to Jacob Böhme emerges in the discussion of the dialectical character of reality.[15]

Tillich's analysis of the demonic ranges from its form-denying and form-creating expressions in Western art through primitive and Asian cultural artifacts, which appear grotesque to the Western mind, to its highest expression in the spiritual lives of individuals. In every expression it is the dialectical quality that gives the demonic its power and depth. He traces the struggle with the demonic through different expressions of religious life and notes the modern tendency to eliminate consciousness of the demonic. Yet, he argues that only when the union of form-creation and form-destruction is seen as the source of demonic power, is a correct analysis of society possible. So, in his discussion of the demonic in society, Tillich acknowledges that social analysis also must be done symbolically and with symbols that have their origins in religious language.

In the *Systematic Theology* the expression of demonry most often discussed is the openly demonic claim of something finite to be holy. The churches are constantly tempted by subtle forms of demonry as they tend to make particularized expressions of religious insight absolute. This analysis of the demonic, which is central to Tillich's total theology, is consistent with his writing about political demonry in 1926. In both cases finite being was, in expressing its form, attempting to claim the infinity of all being, and that drive forced it to destroy its own meaning.

Class Struggle

The profundity of Tillich's social philosophy in this period of cultural reaction is easily appreciated in his essay "Christianity and Modern Society."[16] He recognizes that people are, in large part, the society in which they live. He sees modern, Western society as tending toward an autonomous, secular society living off of its Christian roots. Catholicism in 1928 seemed disconnected from modern life, and Protestantism in both its Lutheran and Reformed manifestations was culturally conservative and therefore uncreative. The conflict between the middle class and the proletariat was the clash of greatest tension and, consequently, of greatest opportunity.[17]

The Reformed support of bourgeois control of society and the Lutheran alliance with the German National party were signs of the religious dimension of the struggle. Yet, the controlling forces were secular. Tillich, in recognizing the importance of the secular society and the autonomous human being of the twentieth century, never surrendered to the forces of the secular. Religion for him was not a term to despise. Only in a new synthesis of religion and society could meaning be found. Religious socialism, though weak, was working at the right issues. It could not realize the new society, but it could struggle against the demonic and point to the need for a "form of grace" in which a new relationship of Christianity and society could emerge.

Tillich's essay on the class struggle casts light on why he delayed joining the Social Democratic party until 1929, when he joined for practical political reasons rather than theoretical agreement.[18] The SPD had become revisionist in its theoretical stance to the neglect of the concept of the class struggle, and for Tillich, the class struggle was the central concept of socialism. In capitalist society previous provisions for security were shattered, and the workers existed in conditions of frightful insecurity. For reasons beyond their control, they were deprived of their work, which was essential to their meaning and being. Members of the proletariat were without means of human fulfillment. There was practically no chance of the proletarian escaping the cycle of unemployment and poverty. The workers came to realize that of the goods they produced they were given those of least value, including poor quality public services, for example, in streets, schools, and protection.

Tillich argues that in this situation, characterized by hopelessness, the workers become aware of living in the midst of meaninglessness. He concludes that the fate of the proletarian is: "isolation, antagonism, and struggle."[19]

For Tillich the concept of class struggle explains the pathos of the proletarian, and at the same time, denies the essential myth of capitalist society. The existence of the class struggle refutes the ideas of social progress for the workers, which were articulated by bourgeois ideologists. The myth of the harmony of bourgeois society is dispelled by the class struggle.

The religious significance of the idea of the class struggle rests in its recognition of the capitalist threat to human meaning. The class struggle concept combines elements of faith in an eventual fulfillment with a demand to act against the demonic forces that enslave the workers. In the essay on the class struggle and religious socialism, Tillich throws his weight against Hendrik de Man's interpretation of socialism as a movement of ethics and education. He explicitly attacks all who would articulate religious socialism bereft of the conception of the class struggle. To deny the class struggle is, for Tillich, to miss the point of socialism.

While his society drifted to the right in politics, Tillich identified himself with a Marxist interpretation of the class struggle. His reservations about the Marxist interpretation were that Marx ended the dialectics of history with the revolution. For Tillich, the dialectics would continue with fulfillment in moments of overcoming the demonic, but not in any perfect realization of the classless society. On religious grounds he was more realistic than Marx.

VII.
The Social Context of the Frankfurt School

As professor of philosophy at the University of Frankfurt (1929–1933), Paul Tillich was closely associated with the membership of the *Institut für Sozialforschung*. The institute was dedicated to social research and the development of a critical theory of society. Its membership was leftist-Hegelian, or humanist-Marxist, in inspiration, and to the left of the Social Democrats in politics.

Tillich's relationship to the *Institut für Sozialforschung* is important to an understanding of his social philosophy. His support and encouragement of the critical theory of the institute indicates the type of social theory and research that interested him. Furthermore, Tillich's social theory was always a social product. He worked his ideas out in discussion, and he wrote in loyalty to those with whom he talked. Therefore, the placing of some of Tillich's ideas in the social context of the thinking of this group at the University of Frankfurt helps to explain several important developments in Tillich's thought.

The institute's wrestling with the theory-praxis question and its conclusion to seek truth in theory characterized Tillich's struggles. His own final, relative withdrawal from praxis to write his *Systematic Theology* was a decision understandable in light of the institute's social reality. The movement from Marxist social philosophy to Freudian psychoanalysis was a movement not of a solitary Tillich, but of a social group seeking a synthesis. Tillich's characteristic ways of addressing the issues of utopian thought, anti-Semitism, and economic theory were molded by his discussions with the members of the institute and their associates. Reflection upon the social reality of the institute is one avenue for understanding the Germanic origins of this immigrant's philosophy of culture and religion and its impact upon North America.

Though it cooperated with the University of Frankfurt, the institute was independently endowed and this independence from state, university, and private capital enabled it to proceed in its own fashion to develop its critical theory. Those attracted to the institute were in large measure Marxists who could support neither the Communist line as practiced in Russia nor the socialism of the Weimar Republic in its diluted trade unionist and practical political form.[2] Rather, they undertook to reform the intellectual roots of Marxism, withdrawing from political realities and seeking their inspiration in empirical research and the philosophy of the young Marx.

Independence from outside contact was, however, alienation from responsibility for society. Tillich was more involved in active socialist politics than were most members of the institute, who were distant from the push and shove of responsible politics. They were closer to Max Weber's "ethic of absolute ends" than to the ethic of responsibility. They understood themselves as critical scholars of politics, not as politicians, and as scholars, their primary form of praxis was critical theory.[3]

Tillich was close friends of three leaders of the institute: Max Horkheimer (director from 1929), Leo Lowenthal, and Friedrich Pollock. Together with Karl Mannheim, Kurt Riezler, Adolph Löwe, and Karl Mennicke, they formed a *Kränzchen,* or intimate discussion group.[3] The group, which was of importance to Tillich's thought, was often hosted by him, first in Frankfurt and later in exile in New York City.

Tillich was at the height of his German academic career as professor of philosophy in Frankfurt. At forty-three years of age his influence was widely felt, and he and Hannah Tillich lived a brilliant and exciting life in Frankfurt.[4] There were frequent dinners and parties and continuous discussion about the social situation, with Karl Mannheim, Erich Fromm, Herbert Marcuse, and Max Horkheimer joining the debate. After 1930 the shadows began to deepen, and cultural expressions turned more to nihilism. Aryan-Semitic disputes began to fracture the university. The Tillichs' friendships were largely among Jewish intellectual circles.[5] Hannah relates that Tillich was in jest referred to as "Paulus among the Jews." Their families and friends came to divide among those supporting the Nazis and those allied with either the Communists or the Socialists. While attending a Nazi rally, Tillich perceived the demonic in Hitler, and he began his critique of politics, *The Socialist Decision,* which was published in January, 1933, and then suppressed.

With the political deterioration of 1932, panic ensued among the Frankfurt circle. The pace of life became faster as if all of life had to be lived before the end. Paul Tillich was among the first university professors to be suspended by the Nazi regime. Of the twelve suspended at Frankfurt on April 13, 1933, one was Tillich and the other eleven were Jewish. He considered the underground, but friends advised him against it. Horkheimer feared that Tillich's hopes for a change in the German situation would cause him to linger too long and result in his death. In fact, in February he had read Tillich a line from one of his writings and told him that if he would not leave Germany, it would cost him his life.[6] After his suspension, Tillich toured the country pondering his decision, and in Dresden he missed arrest by the Gestapo only by a friend's forewarning. He and Hannah prepared to leave Germany, but still Tillich hesitated. Finally, realizing that no academic appointment was possible without recantation of his work, he had a final interview with the Nazi secretary of education. The secretary's responses to Tillich's queries about the Jews and modern culture were unsatisfying. The secretary suggested Tillich leave Germany.[7] The decision was made.

Tillich's years at Frankfurt came to an end through an act of political power. The power that suspended and eventually dismissed him was the power he had analyzed and resisted. Friends in New York, particularly Horace Friess of Columbia University and Reinhold Niebuhr of Union Theological Seminary, had seen the danger, and they secured him an academic appointment at Union. Friess met the Tillichs when their ship docked. Ursula Niebuhr helped them settle into their first apartment in Knox Hall, part of the Union

Seminary quadrangle on 122nd Street near the corner of Broadway. Soon the *Institut für Sozialforschung* was to join them in exile in its new home at Columbia University just across Broadway. In 1931 as the political situation grew more hostile, the institute had established its endowment abroad to provide for its possible continuation outside Germany. Tillich had made many contributions to the Institute. He had helped found a chair of social philosophy for Max Horkheimer to fill when Horkheimer assumed the directorship.[8] He had assisted Theodore Adorno in securing his first position at Frankfurt. He shared with Mannheim, Horkheimer, and Sinzheimer the dismissal from the university. Later, in June, 1949, he urged the institute's reestablishment in Frankfurt, hoping to renew social research and modern social science in Germany.[9]

Through its research, publication, and conversation, the institute created a model of social reality that is reflected in several areas of Tillich's thought. The model, which represented the personalities and minds of the members of the institute, can be seen in: the critical distance of philosophy from practical politics, the combination of Freud and Marx, the problem of utopian reflection, and the economic theory.

Critical Distance

In intellectual heritage and sociological position, Tillich shared the position of the leading members of the institute. This location in the broad spectrum of Left Hegelian–young Marxist thought and their position as the academic elite of Frankfurt kept most of them from active commitment to political parties. In the thirties the proletariat was not behaving according to Marxist philosophy, and the wrath of "les petite bourgeoisie" was about to make the location of the institute in Germany impossible. They were the alienated intellectuals. Tillich voted socialist, and in 1929 he joined the Social Democratic party, but the compromises of the socialist government kept him from enthusiastically endorsing it. The awkwardness of the Communists kept him out of their circles. When he published his major work in politics, *The Socialist Decision,* it called for sophisticated reforms in socialism that the socialist leaders were intellectually and sociologically incapable of making.

Critical theory as represented by Horkheimer, Adorno, and Marcuse was suspicious of finished political-philosophical systems. The work of their school of thought was in large part a critique of the intellectual tradition. Tillich shared their suspicion of existing systems, but he labored to produce a new synthesis, labors that in Germany went largely unnoticed. His *System of the Sciences* received very few reviews. *The Socialist Decision* was consumed by the Nazi holocaust. His first volume of *Systematic Theology,* announced for 1927, did not appear until 1951, and then it lacked the thorough analysis of religious symbol and political philosophy that had been promised in the description for the 1927 volume. Fromm and Marcuse were to contribute their works of synthesis in the United States in their unification of Freudian and Marxian perspectives. Tillich's work in the U.S. would incorporate the Freudian perspective more and more into his theological synthesis, while playing down the Marxian elements. With the gradual discrediting in his mind of neo-Marxist philosophy, however, his final synthetic works of philosophical theology would not have a totally integrated political philosophy. The critical transcendence that characterized the Frankfurt school's politics while Tillich was there was finally dominant in his major work.

Psychoanalysis

Tillich's closest friends were all involved in psychoanalysis and /or the relationship of sociological theory to Freudian theory. In the early 1930s it was intellectually radical, almost academically taboo, to relate Marxism and Freudianism. Neither Communism nor the psychoanalytic movement would touch the synthesis. Nevertheless, those at the institute went ahead, merging Freud and Marx. They perceived problems with Marxism that seemed insolvable without new resources. For his work in getting the Frankfurt Psychoanalytic Institute tied to the University of Frankfurt, Horkheimer received appreciative letters from Freud.[10]

Erich Fromm eventually moved to reject crucial components of Freud's theory, including aspects of the concept of libido.[11] Marx came to play a much larger role in Fromm's thought. He opted for Marx's view of possible human reconciliation and gradually shook off Freudian pessimism. As a result, he was dismissed by the International Psychoanalytic Association and regarded as a revisionist. Differences about Freud among Adorno, Fromm, Horkheimer, and Marcuse did not become apparent until after their emigration. In America, Horkheimer attacked Fromm's revisionism, arguing that Freud's sociological setting in bourgeois Vienna was not necessarily detrimental to his theory. Freud was correct that psychology was intended to focus on the individual, not society, Horkheimer contended, and the libido was a necessary concept. Reconciliation could not precede social reconstruction; theory could not be complete until social contradictions were resolved.[12]

Marcuse's use of Freud to correct Marx followed his disappointment over the purges of Stalin and the cruelties of the Spanish Civil War.[13] In *Eros and Civilization,* he presented Freud as a revolutionary utopian.[14] The debate between Marcuse and Fromm, whose critique was thorough-going, ranged over issues of exegesis of Freud, the character of civilization, the possibility of integrated personalities, the nature of love, and the meaning of tolerance. The issues of the institute of the thirties were to continue to boil over into the United States of the sixties and seventies.

Tillich's move from Marx toward Freud was a move within a community of scholars. It was not simply a retreat from politics, but a way of becoming more critical of politics. There is a book still to be written on Tillich's use of psychoanalytic categories and on the scores of lectures on mental health that he delivered in the 1950s and 1960s in the United States.[15] It should be noted, however, that Tillich, like most other intellectuals, would respond to an invitation to lecture on a subject that was within his range of interest and competence. The fact that he lectured on psychology and used more Freudian terminology is due in large part to American disinterest in Marxian terminology and social revolution. In his preface to *Eros and Civilization,* Marcuse indicated his indebtedness to Max Horkheimer and the institute for his theoretical position and began: "This essay employs psychological categories because they have become political categories." This insight was one of the institute's contributions to Tillich's thought, also.

Utopia

Fromm's thought contained progressive utopian elements that distinguished his work from the critical, negative character of the work of the institute. The scholars associated with the institute, especially Benjamin, Horkheimer, and Adorno, used their utopian visions as principles of critique of the present, not as plans for the future. There was a deep note of pessimism in their work, which Tillich shared.

Utopian hopes kept history moving and negated the need for a mythological glorification of the present. Utopia, related to the prophetic spirit, confronted the "is" with an "ought." Tillich died in 1965, so we cannot know his reaction to the neo-Marxist activism of the late sixties. He opposed similar activism in the 1930s, however, looking for a middle way. Adorno expressed his dismay that much of the ideological fervor of the activists of the sixties came from the theoretical work of the institute. Martin Jay argued that Adorno's regrets pointed to "a fundamental conclusion of the theory itself: negation could never be truly negated."[16] With the dissolution of the proletariat, utopia had only a critical function.

For Tillich, finally: *"it is the spirit of utopia that conquers utopia."*[17] (Tillich's italics.) This means that utopia is distinguished from the Kingdom of God. Tillich's statement contains the idea that there are particularly significant times in history in which much can be accomplished. It also and most forcefully means that the freedom of the human spirit is such that no form of human organization will fulfill it. The human spirit is truly led to strive beyond its present boundaries, but while the Kingdom of God may be realized momentarily in human history as the vertical dimension intersects the horizontal dimension, fulfillment is never complete. Life continues as a tragic-ironic existence in which the critical function must be practiced.

Economics

Economics was never of independent, isolated concern to Tillich. The discipline was important as it related to humanistic needs, and the ethical and psychological implications of economics interested him. Tillich stood in debt to both Marx and Freud, and like his friend Herbert Marcuse, he synthesized these perspectives into his own. An example of the tensions in thought produced by this synthesizing is available for examination in *The Protestant Era*. On one page, he wrote:

> The economic sphere is the most important historical factor —not in all times, as some dogmatic Marxists assert—but certainly within bourgeois capitalism.[18]

However, on the very next page, his psychological interest became apparent:

> But more important than the immediate economic consequences of the monopolistic stage of liberal economy are its psychological effects on the masses.[19]

These two claims for importance do not contradict each other, but they show the tension between a Marxist claim for the centrality of economics and a Freudian tendency to focus on the psychological state of the masses. Recognizing the tension, Tillich wrote: "These effects have created a revolutionary situation in the whole Western world."[20] This acknowledgment of both psychological and economic sources of political change is characteristic of Tillich and his friends associated with the critical theory of the Frankfurt School. It was not necessarily an anti-Marxist move in scholarship—since some scholars today would regard it as a proper development of Marx's own insights—but such work, before the views of Fromm and Marcuse became accepted, was quite radical and controversial.

In response to Clark A. Kucheman's critical essay from a capitalist perspective on his socialism, Tillich again indicated the subordination of economics to humanist concerns in his thought.

> In the most extended description of my social-political ideas, the book *Die Sozialistische Entscheidung,* I have developed a many-sided image of a transformed society in which the economic element is definitively subordinated.[21]

Tillich's ideas about economics can only be grasped in his broadened humanistic perspective. In his view of a transformed order, which is basically socialist, some feudal and bourgeois elements remain.

Certain ideas about the economic order that were Marxist in inspiration disappeared from his writing and speaking after World War II. These ideas are present in the original edition of *The Protestant Era,* but absent or muted in the abridged edition and lacking from later speeches and writing on society. The social context in which he worked changed. The "controlled capitalism" of the United States, with its powerful trade union movement, was not the Berlin of the interwar period. The concept of the proletariat was obsolete in the U.S. The problems of social injustice in the United States, primarily those of poverty and race, were problems of dehumanization, which were not best addressed by the categories of early twentieth-century German religious socialism.

It was irrelevant to contend in the United States that the masses were becoming more impoverished, or that the increase of "unproductive capital in the banks"[22] drove the country into imperialism and war, or that the rapidity of technological advance demanded by capitalism would necessarily mean increasing structural unemployment, or that the proletariat was a revolutionary vanguard. However, the weakening of the persuasiveness of some of Marx's economic ideas did not allow his thought to be confined to the past. It had influenced modern thinking to the extent that an analysis of capitalist society without reference to Marxian thought was unlikely to be productive. Tillich did not want to return to the illusions of harmony in the marketplace, or to justify contemporary democracies on the basis of an idealism of progress.[23]

Tillich knew the extent to which the workers in the Berlin suburbs had been reduced in many aspects of their being to a mass level. The system of production—which included a standardization of work, a standardization of a low wage, a uniformity of housing opportunities, and a sameness of education to prepare them for industry—determined their lives. Tillich thought Marx was right to emphasize that the system of material production was fundamental; however, he criticized Marxists who would simply deduce all aspects of culture from the system of production. To the extent that Marx rigidly deduced the superstructure from the substructure of production, Tillich was critical of his theory, also:

The economic sphere is itself a complex sphere, to which all other spheres essentially contribute, so that they cannot be derived from it, although they can never be separated from it.[24]

In economics, as elsewhere, Tillich's direct dependence on members of his discussion circle was acknowledged. Eduard Heimann and Adolf Löwe, who had been members of his Kairos Circle in Berlin, for example, were the sources of the economic theory in *The Socialist Decision*. The setting of economic reflections in the broad social context was, again, a characteristic of the Frankfurt School.

VIII.
The Socialist
Decision

Tillich's mature, socialist political philosophy is best represented in *The Socialist Decision.* [1] By the time he signed the foreword to the volume in November, 1932, in Frankfurt, he had lived fourteen years as a socialist. His youthful enthusiasm for the socialism of the November, 1918, revolution had sobered. He knew well the failures and confusions in theory and practice of the socialism of the Weimar Republic. He had taught social philosophy as well as become a leading religious, socialist essayist. In only a few months, he would be suspended with eleven Jewish colleagues from the University of Frankfurt where his radicalism had been nurtured in the Frankfurt School. The only rival to first place for significance in Tillich's political philosophy is the later *Love, Power, and Justice,* but *The Socialist Decision* has an immediacy to its abstract political philosophy that *Love, Power, and Justice* lacks. To some degree the categories of meaning are more refined in *Love, Power, and Justice,* but the socialist passion that informs *The Socialist Decision* is absent, or only implied. The later volume represents Tillich's political philosophy without a program; *The Socialist Decision* includes a program, which subsequently leads to his exile.

Tillich's motivations for publishing *The Socialist Decision* are helpful background to the interpretation of the work. A motivation that remained unmentioned, but which was always in the background of

Tillich's work, was the need for expression of his deeply speculative mind. Another motivation was to bring together countless conversations, many lectures, and earlier partial works into a new whole and give expression to his deep political commitments. A third motivation for its publication was to respond to the political situation of 1932. A A philosopher could best fight romantic reaction by philosophizing, so Tillich put his mind into the political struggle. The Social Democratic party was becoming increasingly enfeebled as it moved out of the governing coalition and then saw its base in the industrial proletariat being eroded. The growing strength of capitalist and feudal elements in German society was threatening. The international situation was foreboding. But foremost in Tillich's mind was fear of the rising National Socialism and the specter of chaos that its impending victory heralded. National Socialism is identified on the second page of the work, and the possibility of luring the revolutionary elements away from Nazism is the variable upon which hope for socialism rests in the conclusion to the work.

To be understood, therefore, *The Socialist Decision* must be seen not as a work focusing on political economy, but as a work of speculative, critical, constructive, polemical, political philosophy. In Tillich's mind, Nazism should be criticized fundamentally by attacking its roots rather than its outrages. He convincingly demonstrates in this work the impossibility of Nazi thought and thereby does what he can as philosopher to kill it before it comes to political power. In this action of the mind, as elsewhere, he was radical to the core. The earliness of his radical opposition to the Nazis resulted in his dismissal from the university and his being urged by the government to emigrate. Only a few months later the same work would have resulted in his immediate arrest.

Emphasizing the attack on Nazism can obscure the positive, constructive work of the book. In it, Tillich proposes a reformulation of socialism, which he conceived to draw forces away from National Socialism. He argues for and places his hopes in a revolutionary socialism that could still, in 1932, achieve a victory and govern Germany.

The outline of the volume reveals clearly Tillich's political philosophy. First, he indicates that there are two types of political philosophies: those grounded in myths of origin and those founded in prophetic criticism of those myths. Second, he analyzes political romanticism and the attempt to define political existence as sacred because of its origins in soil, blood, and social group. Third, he discusses Western capitalism as an expression of the attack upon the myths of origin.

The dissolution of all primary ties and the attempt to integrate them into purposeful structures depend upon the myth of harmony. Tillich argues that the myth of harmony has been refuted by contemporary history, exposing instead a world of class conflict and imperialist struggles among capitalist nations. The chaos of contemporary industrial society requires that the myth of harmony be replaced by conscious social planning. The character of the conflicts of capitalist society requires a socialist answer. But unless socialism can provide a new synthesis of the criticism of the myths of origin and connections with the powers of the myths of origin, it cannot compete with political romanticism or liberal capitalism. In the third part of the study, he proposes a reform of socialism that will equip it for the struggle. He exposes socialism as the inheritor of a prophetic criticism that gives way to neither resignation nor utopia, but that unites its social planning with symbols of expectation to transform society.

The strength of political romanticism lay in its attack upon the dehumanizing aspects of modern society. Liberal-rational society had deep problems even when it functioned well economically. In the thirties, however, the humiliation of Germany in international politics and the ravages of depression dealt the modern attempt to build a rational society the death blow. Conservative romantics like Chancellor Franz von Papen were confined to defending islands of tradition in a sea of change. The attacks of the landowners, the Protestant churches, and the old military leadership upon the Weimar Republic undercut it, playing into the hands of the Communists and the Nazis rather than returning modern society to the traditional patterns the conservatives sought. Revolutionary political romanticism inherited a distaste for modern society and combined revolutionary criticism of the present with an apocalyptic hope for a return to mythical origins. This combination of apocalyptic fervor and radical criticism gave Nazism, which was the major expression of political romanticism, a political weapon of great strength, though of limited duration. Apocalyptic political thought may, when expressed in brilliant tactics, gain political power, but it cannot in itself govern.

Critique of Nazism

Tillich's critique of Nazism was devastating, and Hannah Tillich's laughter at reading it was the laughter both of relief that they were to escape the barbarism, and of the defiance of absurd but overwhelming power.[2] A nationalistic German tradition could not endure because there was no national tradition. The tradition of Germany was sectionalism, and if there were any national tradition, it would be the fighting among various sectional traditions.

The return to the myths of origin, with its search for meaning in soil, blood, and social group, was an attempt to eclipse the rational consciousness and to obliterate the distinction between "is" and "ought." It was an attempt to make existence itself sacred and to justify a group by reference to its origins. Return to the soil was not economically feasible, but it attracted some political supporters. Return to one blood was anthropological nonsense, but it built on the anti-Semitism that had been developing in Germany. Also, the appeal to race set the population up for the return to a social group using the model of a patriarchal community dominated by a leader rather than a rational group. Conservative and revolutionary romantics could lust together to overthrow liberal democracy and its bureaucracy even as they dreamed respectively of a monarch or a *Führer*.

Tillich tried to show that political romanticism could not make any headway in the sciences. It could make some gains in poetry, but its real field of persuasive power rested in an ecstatic, revolutionary, agitated apocalypticism. He repeated that there were no theorists worthy of respect in the National Socialist movement. He attacked their piecemeal use of Nietzsche, arguing that Nietzsche proved that anti-Semitism and nationalism were contemptible. Systematic thinking, in Tillich's judgment, was denied and then overthrown by Nazi practice. Nazism did use scientific language as a cover for its apocalyptic message, but in essence it was antiscientific.

Tillich regarded political romanticism in its Nazi form as a religious phenomenon. It was an attempt to create a new system of meaning and salvation by a return to myths of origin without critical inquiry. It was demonic in its attempt to make race, leader, party, and space holy, and there was no way for the church to maintain its integrity but by opposition. He saw the Nazi attempt to seduce church support as one more example of trying to make the new bearer of meaning, the nation, holy by gaining the blessing of the old bearer of meaning, the church. He saw Protestant churches as overly dependent on their supporting groups, unable to present effective resistance because they lacked sociological authority. As it tried to adjust to the new patterns or to escape the pain of relevance by confining its message to the realms of transcendence, Protestantism stood exposed as without significance. Tillich called elsewhere in 1932 for a Protestant critique of National Socialism, but he knew Nazism's sociological condition made significant opposition impossible.[3] He did not foresee that National Socialism would, by its direct attack on the churches, cause some of them to resist National Socialism for the sake of the freedom of the church.

Spirit of Judaism

Though Tillich was not inclined to reduce the significance of National Socialism to anti-Semitism, he regarded the political romanticism of Nazism as essentially opposed to the Jewish spirit. He located the Jewish spirit in the prophets who transcended blood, soil, and communal loyalties in honoring a universal God who judged Israel in terms of justice. The Old Testament itself broke the primitive pagan myths of origin and was, consequently, anathema to Nazism. The spirit of Judaism was inevitably an "eternal adversary of political romanticism." The myth of origin could still be found in biblical Jewish faith, but only in a criticized mode, and it was usually confined to the priestly rather than the prophetic traditions. Christianity belonged plainly on the side of Judaism in this affirmation of a prophetic critique of romanticism and so, especially, did the Reformation.

The ethical monotheism of Judaism shared with the rational Greek philosophy the overcoming of myth. In more modern expression, the Reformation and the Enlightenment carried on the fight against uncriticized myths of origin. Political romanticism could best be understood as a countermovement against the prophetic in religion and the humanistic in culture. In Judaism the German primitive mythology of blood and race found both a discordant factual reality and a sharp ideological critique.

Tillich, of course, had many of his closest friendships with Jewish philosophers and scientists. He worked with Jewish intellectuals in Frankfurt, and he shared the early dismissal from the University of Frankfurt with his Jewish colleagues. His wartime participation in the Council for a Democratic Germany had as one of its goals continuing support for persecuted Jews, and in New York he continually found himself allied with Jewish causes. He came to abandon as inappropriate, Christian attempts to convert Jews, but continued to engage in dialogue with them about the Christ as well as politics. As a member of the American Palestine Committee, he adopted a position that can be regarded as a form of Christian support for Zionism. The full story of Tillich's support for Judaism is discussed in the final chapter; the important point here is that Judaism shared with Protestantism and humanism the essential rejection of primitive myths of origin, and it was the first to bear the brunt of Nazism's wrath.

Socialism

Socialism meant to Tillich a manner of organizing society that merged the religious values of the myths of origin with the prophetic critique of those myths in a rational-cooperative social order. He had described the sterility and ruthless competitiveness of the capitalist order in an earlier work that appeared in the United States in translation as *The Religious Situation*. [4] Its basic point was that while capitalism was essentially a war of all against all in both the domestic and the international political economy, the capitalists disguised the conflict with the myth of laissez-faire harmony and a theory of the balance of power in European politics. In the twenties and thirties, it had become increasingly obvious that a social model of class and national conflict was more adequate than a myth of harmony. International war and class warfare gave the lie to capitalist mythology. The secondary aspect of Tillich's critique of the spirit of capitalism was that it produced a sterility of human character in its ruthless pursuit of rationalized profit-taking and social dislocation in the exploited classes. Tillich's argument in 1932 made use of the then recently discovered early manuscripts of Karl Marx on economic and philosophical issues, and he joined Marx in attacking the alienation of life produced by the capitalist order.

Tillich was not a devotee of political parties, as we have seen, but in the early excitement of the 1918 revolution he had associated with the radical Independent Social Democrats, and in 1929 he joined the regular Social Democratic party. By 1932, with the Social Democrats out of power, he thought they could finally surrender the elements of bourgeois thought that they had been forced to accept as partners in the government of the Weimar Republic. His writing in that year was an attempt to radicalize the Social Democrats, while at the same time emphasizing the universal elements of socialism to gain it a larger political base.

Socialism had both particular and universal aspects. The particular rested in its dependence upon the radicalness of the proletarian movement. Its universal side rested in its hopes of ending the proletarian situation by creating an order freed from the negative features of a class society. He resisted giving up the particular elements, trying instead to recruit forces to socialism by emphasizing its universal side.

He believed that his contribution as a socialist philosopher and as an ideologist within socialist discussion groups was to show how the inner conflicts[5] of socialist theory could be overcome. He found these conflicts in six areas: (1) the socialist creed, (2) the conception of humanity, (3) the conception of society, (4) the conception of culture, (5) the idea of community, and (6) the theory of economy.

The first and second conflicts blended into one and presented the fundamental problem of Marxist theory: How is a group of people, the exploited proletariat, both to be determined by material conditions and to become the vanguard of the new society? Tillich believed that early philosophic manuscripts of Marx contained the solution to the problem. If society could be made conscious of the solution, Marxism would reveal the essentially religious nature of its hopes. Socialism must be understood as essentially prophetic; that is, it perceives immanent possibilities within the exploited proletariat that can be realized through the demand for justice. Socialism cannot remain in a position of dogmatic resignation or become utopian. It must, through the correct reading of the possibilities inherent in the proletariat, confess that it is calling for a transformation of human nature as it is expressed existentially in society. Socialism's principle is not that of a materialistic resignation, but rather that of the *symbol of expectation*. There is within the proletariat a human element that is not reduced by the process of capitalist "thingification." Given a promise of hope, but not of utopia, the proletariat can become active and determinative of historical destiny in this epoch. The prophetic element contained within socialism fights against the oppression of the poor and threatens the nation with destruction because of its injustice. Tillich's socialism is similar to some strands of the theologies of hope and revolution of the seventies, as well as directly dependent upon the Old Testament prophets. Socialism expresses a demand for the transformation of the proletarian situation into a truer expression of human nature. A political eschatology, then, is the essence of the socialist principle for Tillich.

The first conflict, which had forced socialism to sound utopian, is attacked by a discovery of the prophetic base of socialism. The second, in the doctrine of humanity, is resolved by understanding that the material base of human existence as proletariat is transformed by conscious human action in the direction of justice.

The third conflict lay in the ability of the socialists to use power to conquer power for the sake of renouncing power. The Social Democrats of the Weimar Republic had not exercised effective use of the instruments of power at their disposal. The overreliance on liberal theories concerning the importance of democracy had deluded them into thinking that socialism could prevail by purely parliamentary means. Tillich had detailed his own theory of power in the *Neue Blätter* in 1931, and he drew upon it in *The Socialist Decision*. He criticized socialism's tendencies toward powerless utopian views. He treated democratic government as a corrective of social tendencies and as an agency to be used in correcting an unjust society, but it was not the essence of society. Democracy had to be limited on the one hand so that the social order could be reconstituted, and radicalized on the other hand so that a social-economic democracy could be realized. Socialism had to be clearer in articulating how its revolutionary impetus **was** based in the struggle for justice, but, at the same time, remain free to exercise power against the structures of government that protected class interest.

The inner conflicts of socialism regarding culture reflected socialist dependence upon the spirit of capitalist society. The socialist tendency to regard religion as a private affair placed it within the bourgeois-liberal position of granting toleration to religion and denying its relevance. Socialism had ended up affirming materialism, liberalism, and atheism, while the Protestant churches were defending idealism, orthodoxy, and authoritarian religion. Socialism did not need to remain in a French-revolutionary attitude of bourgeois rejection of religion. Rather, it needed to discover the religious elements in its own consciousness and reveal that its essence was not antispiritual. The scientific approach of socialism was not necessarily antireligious, for science was antireligious only to people who were of a nonscientific mind themselves. Socialism understood at its roots was religious, and it needed to work out an accord between its secular symbolism and its religious symbolism.

The conflict of socialism concerning national community needed to be overcome if socialism were to prevail. Nationalism in its Nazi or Junker reactionary forms was demonic, but the importance of loyalties to soil, blood, tradition, and social group had to be taken seriously. Socialism suffered because it was regarded as an international conspiracy. The internationalism or universalism of socialism was a fact rooted in the transnational interests of the proletariat and the need for an international order. But its particularism, as expressed in particular national loyalties, was also a fact. The prophetic spirit of socialism proceeded toward humanity but was rooted in the nation and its needs. Tillich, therefore, opted for a localized socialism; in fact, he argued that socialism must affirm the nation more deeply than any nationalist ideology. That meant that the affirmation of the nation must always be under the unconditional demands of justice. Tillich's appreciation of power—an element of his faithful realism—demanded the conclusion that socialism had to be realized one nation at a time. Though he did not develop a complete socialist social ethic, Tillich pointed to the need for the development of such an ethic, which would make clear how socialism could further the liberation of women and the empowerment of minorities within a nation-state.

The final conflict that demanded resolution was in the area of economics. Depending largely on the already published economic writings of Adolf Löwe and Eduard Heimann, Tillich resisted options in socialism that completely abolished private property and subjected the economy to total centralization. He thought aspects of the free market, involving principles of supply and demand, and the marginal utility principle for fixing the correlation of need and price had to be maintained.

He argued for state central planning that would make the crucial investment decisions and assimilate all income into centralized decision making. The areas to be nationalized included the great centers of real property, heavy industry, centers of manufacturing, banking, and foreign trade. In other areas a relatively free economy could be maintained. He argued against the total bureaucratic state, which would swamp all initiative in red tape.

Against the distorted version of the Protestant work ethic, he argued that work was not religion and certainly not salvation. There was no religious justification for the cause of work that resulted in senseless slavery to the machine and the goals of technology. Technology was to be justified through its submission to human needs as adjudicated through the political process and central planning. The goal of the socialist economy was the rational utilization of earthly possibilities for human development, first on a national basis and, eventually, on a global basis.

In his conclusion to *The Socialist Decision,* Tillich argued that the struggle between political romanticism and bourgeois liberalism would lead to chaos: The victory of bourgeois liberalism would continue the present chaos, and if political romanticism captured the rampant nationalism of the time, there would be war and then chaos. Only in a socialism using the revolutionary elements within liberalism and political romanticism could he see an escape from social disintegration, defeat, and chaos.[6] But in 1932 it was already too late. The politics of the Social Democrats were played out. Socialism was unable to reform itself, and chaos and war followed.

IX.
Between
Two Worlds
1933~1938

The year 1933 tore apart German society and shattered the existence of Paul Tillich. He was overrun by the dynamism of Hitler's multilevel attack on the meaning of Germany. Heinrich Heine had written:

> Christianity—and this is its fairest merit—subdued to a certain extent the brutal warrior ardour of the Germans but it could not entirely quench it; and when the cross, that restraining talisman, falls to pieces, then will break forth again the ferocity of the old combatants, the frantic Berserker rage whereof Northern poets have said and sung so much. The talisman has become rotten, and the day will come when it will pitifully crumble to dust. The old stone gods will arise then from the forgotten ruins and wipe from their eyes the dust of centuries, and Thor with his giant hammer will arise again, and he will shatter the Gothic cathedrals. . . .[1]

Heine, a Jew, had prophesied correctly. Cathedrals and all they stood for would be broken.

Hitler overcame his opponents with ruthlessness and dynamism. He used the legal forms of society to capture the society, and then he destroyed those forms. Though the Nazi party had declined in voting strength from the summer to the fall of 1933, it was still the strongest party. Wishful thinking and Communist collaboration in overthrowing the Weimar coalition paved the way for Hindenburg's appointment of Hitler as head of the government on January 30, 1933. Events followed quickly: The Reichstag fire of February 28 led to the granting of emergency powers. The Enabling Act of March 24 made Hitler virtual dictator. The one-day boycott of Jewish business followed in April. The trade unions were abolished in May. The other political parties were proscribed in July, and the revolutionaries within the Nazi party—the S.A. headed by Ernst Röhm—were suppressed in June and July. The Vatican agreed to the dismantling of its political opportunities in the Concordat of July. New elections for the Protestant churches gave the "German Christians" a temporary victory in July and church resistance to Hitler stiffened, but by that time it was the only institution offering resistance. President Hindenburg's death in August, 1934, completed the Nazi takeover with Hitler assuming the offices of both president and chancellor. Overthrown in this rush of events was university life, the primary context of Paul Tillich's life.

Opposition and Exile

As the dean of the philosophical faculty, Tillich was thrust into the turmoil. He demanded the expulsion of Nazi students who joined with storm troopers to terrorize the university. He was bitterly attacked in the *Frankfurter Zeitung,* and passages from *The Socialist Decision* were quoted to prove him an enemy of the new order. His suspension from the University of Frankfurt on April 13, 1933, was as a suspect intellectual and a member of the SPD.

Tillich's eventual dismissal was because of his role as a socialist theoretician, but he had also opposed Nazism on theological grounds. In 1932 he had published "Ten Theses on the Church and the Third Reich." The theses were published in a book entitled *The Church and the Third Reich: Questions and Demands of German Theologians.* The volume, first of two published by Leopold Klotz to stimulate debate over Nazism, was sent to Hitler. One of Hitler's professors, J. Stark, attacked the book:

> "The book in question affords a valuable commentary on the intellectual level of numerous 'evangelical' academic theolo-

gians. Never have I seen such an accumulation of ignorance, superficiality, presumption, and malicious enmity to the German Freedom Movement."[2]

Tillich's sentences bristled with theological polemic. A Protestantism that opened itself to Nazism but closed itself to socialism betrayed its mission to the world. The Protestant churches, apparently honoring the text "The Kingdom of God is not of this world," had surrendered to the demons of the victorious political powers. The justifying of the Nazi mythology of blood and race was a retreat to paganism and a denial of God and humanity. By supporting the capitalist interests of Nazism, the church gave up its quest for justice. Current Protestantism lacked a principle of creative social criticism because it had not maintained a vision of the Kingdom of God; consequently, it was subject to control by the same social groups supporting Nazism. The neutrality proclamation of the church was a sham because opponents of Nazism found no support while the church attacked socialism. Protestantism could prove its worth by standing against the heathenism of the swastika and for the cross, which breaks false claims to authority. Protestants ought to be free to join all political parties, and all political parties must be criticized by a prophetic understanding of the Kingdom of God. Keeping politics under criticism could show the aspects of the groups supporting Nazism that were genuine while freeing the groups from the fluctuating control of the demonic. The hidden alliance of Protestantism with Nazism would lead to the disintegration of Protestantism.[3]

Tillich's opposition to Nazism was unequivocal. It was grounded in his theology and his socialism and in his synthesis of the two in his political theology. The Nazis suspended him and burned his book in the square in Frankfurt. He did, however, equivocate about leaving Germany. Friends were emigrating and friends advised him to leave. Events rushed in upon him. The ability of the Nazis to remain in power was not clear to him. He began preparations to leave Germany while still seeking an option to stay. The invitation from Union Theological Seminary to come to New York seems to have been the deciding event. Without the invitation to continue his

work abroad, he might have stayed, and such a delay might have
been fatal. At the ministry of education, he was warned to leave and
to remain out of Germany. Even from New York, he tried to retain
his Frankfurt professorship, but his appeals were in vain. By the end
of 1933, his suspension was made an official dismissal.

Soon Tillich's apartment at Union Theological Seminary became
a center for refugees from Germany. Friendships were renewed,
politics were discussed, and arrangements to assist other refugees
were made. In November, 1936, the organization Self-Help for
Emigrés from Central Europe was created, and Tillich became its
chairman. He labored for the agency for fifteen years as organizer,
counselor, and philosopher. The organization was kept open and
flexible to be able to respond creatively and immediately to need.[4]

Gradually Tillich came to find meaning in forced emigration and
exile. He came to understand emigration as the way that God shattered human securities and so allowed mankind to respond in faith:
If God elected people, he separated them from old customs and
mores. Abraham became archetypical for the experiences of emigration. God chose Abraham for a special destiny and forced him to
emigrate. So, too, Israel had to emigrate to Egypt and back, to
Babylon and back, and into exile in the Western world. Christians
were emigrants, separated from both Judaism and paganism.

Tillich came to understand emigration not as cruel fate, but as a
religious category for understanding reality. It witnessed to the ex-
clusiveness of God and to the relativity of all human bonds. By 1936
he could address a group of refugees and say:

> Emigration by itself is a protest against the nationalistic distor-
> tion of Christianity and defamation of humanity. The support
> of emigrés is a support of prophetic protest against the de-
> monic energy of religious nationalism.[5]

He concluded with an appeal to support emigration whether out of
Christian love, moral outrage, or for political reasons; but he reminded his audience that there was an ultimate religious truth in the
experience of emigration.

Struggle within the Church

Most Protestant clergy welcomed Hitler's rise to power in 1933, though divisions among the Nazi supporters soon became clear. There were the conservative German Christians, many of whom were united in the *Christlich-Deutsche Bewegung* (CDB). This group was "closer to the Nationalist Party (DNVP)"[6] than to the National Socialists. The CDB attempted to maintain a moderate position of support for Hitler while retaining theological integrity. It folded before the end of 1933, and the more enthusiastic supporters of Nazism moved into the *Glaubensbewegung Deutsche Christen* (GDC). Emmanuel Hirsch was one of the few nationally known theologians who joined the GDC, along with Paul Althaus and Friedrich Wienke. The GDC was created by the Nazis. It did not have the academic prestige of the CDB, but it was more enthusiastic and committed to the religious-political struggle. Ideology and theology were surrendered in this group to the Nazi attempt to control the church. Hitler supported the GDC in the church elections of July, 1933, when the enthusiasm for a unified church supporting Hitler crested. A third group, the *Kirchenbewegung Deutsche Christen* (KDC), was the most ideologically consistent with Nazism. This group originated in Thuringia in 1927 and represented anti-Semitism and devotion to blood, soil, and *Volk* in their most vehement forms.

After 1933 the Nazis were unable to control the church. Most theologians withdrew from the GDC and gradually repented of their earlier support of Nazi efforts to capture the church. The movement for a German Christianity operated without Hitler's support, and church affairs were reduced to chaos. The German Christian movement, however, continued under various names and in different alliances. Hirsch, Tillich's friend from the university days, remained committed to the German Christian cause until the end of the war, and his attempt to provide a theology for the movement elicited Tillich's attack upon him in 1935.

Hirsch had always opposed the Weimar Republic. He had longed for an end to the parliamentary confusion and the mixture of liberalism and Marxism that dominated Germany after the 1918 revolution. He contributed to Christian anti-Semitic tendencies and played down the importance of the Old Testament for Christian theology. His thought rooted in the nationalist idealism of Fichte, Hirsch developed a political theory that deemphasized the state. His basic concept was of a people, or *Volk,* which was created by God. The *Volk* was the bearer of meaning, and when a state did not allow the fulfillment of the *Volk,* it could be overthrown. The revolution he justified was, of course, not the founding revolution of the Weimar Republic, but the one that would replace it.

In 1934 Hirsch had his newly published *The Present Cultural Situation in Philosophical and Theological Perspective* sent to Tillich in New York. Tillich criticized the book in the German journal *Theologische Blätter* in the form of an open letter that mixed personal treatment of the subject with bitter polemic.[7] Hirsch included a response to Tillich in another book, *Christian Freedom and Political Obligation.* Tillich responded again in the *Theologische Blätter,* concluding the discussion.[8]

Though at the beginning of this exchange Tillich indicated his personal friendship for Hirsch, he thought it necessary to refute the principal arguments of *The Present Cultural Situation.* [9] Tillich admitted that Hirsch and other devotees of the German Christian movement were using categories that had been developed within religious socialism, but he deplored the distortion of the categories and Hirsch's refusal to acknowledge the borrowing of certain concepts. Tillich accused Hirsch of borrowing the religious-socialist concepts of "kairos" and "boundary" as well as the general outlines of the intellectual situation. He asserted that Hirsch stood with the young Karl Marx in seeking existential-historical thinking. The essence of Tillich's attack, however, was that in uncritically affirming the changes of 1933, Hirsch had surrendered to the demonic-sacramental forces. He accused Hirsch of giving up his vocation as a Protestant theologian in his enthusiasm for a movement and of considering a finite historical movement as an absolute. The kairos doctrine was thus misused by Hirsch because he ignored the religious reservation about all finite movements. Hirsch forgot the dialectical balance of faithful realism when he was unreservedly critical of the 1918 revolution and unreservedly affirmative of the 1933 revolution.

The theology of Hirsch seemed to make contemporary events revelatory. Tillich admitted that the previous articulation of the kairos doctrine had not been adequately guarded from this misuse, but he argued that revelation is first and it seizes the subject; after that, other events are examined in relationship to the original revelation. An event is "in kairos" only if it corresponds to the original kairos. A new event does not change the meaning of revelation. Kairos by itself is not revelation; rather, it shows a fresh realization of the original revelation. The cross of Christ—and Tillich thanked Hirsch for clarifying this idea for him—is the judge of Hirsch's claim for the "German hour."

Tillich attacked Hirsch for remaining quiet when Jewish businesses were boycotted and for failing to attribute racial legislation, which Hirsch supported, to the simple racial hatred that was infecting Germany. He criticized Hirsch's basic concept of *Volk* as meaningless, representing no more than the current will dominating the German people. He argued that Hirsch had fallen back on primitive sacramental language and had refused to use critical sociological concepts. If there were to be a sacred-blood community as Hirsch argued, asked Tillich, would it not be for a theologian the community of Christian communion? Hirsch's concept of a "concealed sovereignty" in the *Volk,* Tillich criticized, was really no more than a way to avoid the antirevolutionary teaching of Lutheran ethics. It was not a responsible concept of a theology of politics, but only an apology for the Protestant rush to support Hitler.

In the closing section of his first letter, Tillich reminded Hirsch that religious socialism taught not only the need for religious social action, but also the need for a religious reservation about social action. He accused Hirsch of ignoring reservation, falling into an unholy religious enthusiasm for Nazism, and betraying his responsibilities as a theologian.

Tillich's second letter reemphasized this theme, saying that Hirsch had even identified the divine with a human realm. Barth had shown the profanity of the political realm. Tillich, while agreeing with Barth, sought in the doctrine of kairos a middle way, which criticized the sacramental understanding of politics with a prophetic insight, while remaining open to the manifestation of the power of being in historical events. Such manifestations, for Tillich, must be judged by the cross of Christ and the gospel of the coming Kingdom of God. Tillich accused Hirsch of using the two-realm theory of Luther to free the secular realm from prophetic criticism while allowing one to participate in it with religious enthusiasm. Tillich's kairos doctrine was in some ways similar to the two-realm theory of Luther, but it avoided the pitfalls of Hirsch and Barth.

When the Nazi movement tried to capture religious support in 1933, Hirsch fell into the trap. Barth resolutely opposed such a compromise; but in his opposition, he failed to grasp the religious significance of some political moments. Tillich tried to maintain a dialectical approach. Practical politics was of a different order from theological politics. A theology of politics, though, had to take seriously the philosophical claims of political ideology, which often became religious claims. Theology had to evaluate and judge those religious claims. Tillich had been doing this in his lectures at Frankfurt on the political principles of German political parties. Tillich's debate with Hirsch was both political and theological. Politics, however, dominated the practical outcome. Tillich had been driven from Frankfurt by the Nazis. Hirsch would be driven out of the university in 1945 by the victorious allies.[10]

Sounding the Alarm

Tillich returned to Europe in 1936. He spent the spring and summer visiting and lecturing in the United Kingdom, Holland, Belgium, Luxembourg, France, Switzerland, and Italy. His travel diary, which was written for Hannah, makes available more detailed knowledge of these few months of his life than is known about any other period. He minutely recorded foods tasted, wines drunk, strangers encountered, reunions had with friends, conversations held, lectures given, and sites visited. The pages of the diary were mailed to Hannah and intended for her and the family. Its publication five years after his death gives an intimate glimpse into his character.[11]

War clouds were gathering in 1936. Hitler had remilitarized the Rhineland, denounced disarmament pacts, and, in the summer of 1936, joined with Mussolini in the revolution to install fascism in

Spain. Tillich's conversations and lectures in England were designed
to wake the British out of their slumber. He spoke against the
pacifism and self-complacency that prevented the parliamentary society from realizing the danger in which it existed. He often found
himself assailed by the English who were in a mood of appeasement.
While in England, he entertained the idea of joining his friend from
Berlin, Adolf Löwe, at the University of Manchester. The leading
light of the church and society movement in England, John Oldham,
also tried to prevail upon Tillich to stay.

A visit with Reinhold Niebuhr in Switzerland served to deepen
their mutual affection, and Niebuhr advised Tillich to decline the
Manchester offer. According to Tillich, Niebuhr urged him to stay
at Union Theological Seminary, saying, "we will found a school of
theology there."[12] Tillich and Niebuhr were cooperating politically
at the time in the Fellowship of Socialist Christians in the United
States and in trying to awaken Christians in Europe to the imminent
danger. Tillich's decision to stay at Union was to have profound
consequences in American Theology.

During his European tour, Tillich spoke about the Nazi victory
in terms of the disintegration of Western society. He described his
perspective as that of "tragic dialectic." His pessimism drove him to
look for resources of renewal, and he could not find them in the
institutional church or in the other institutions of Western democracy. He called on political and intellectual leaders to covenant
together to analyze the situation and to propose avenues of action.
He described his idea as a religious order, and it merged elements
from his religious-socialist group experience with an almost monastic
retreat from the diseased world so that new proposals for political
action could be engendered.[13] He received polite encouragement
from those with whom he discussed the idea, but the concept bore
little practical fruit. John Oldham did develop a Christian Frontier
Society that had some of the aspects of what he and Tillich discussed
in 1936.[14]

From the Netherlands and from Switzerland, he could actually
see Germany. Family and friends came out to visit him, but even in
his private memoirs there is no hint of a desire to return. Germany
was a prison, and he was free on the outside. He urged other exiles

he met to start a new life abroad. Emotionally, he was not tempted to go home, but he often discussed the possibility of the assassination of Hitler. He regarded the remote possibility of a coup against Hitler and a negotiated settlement of the outstanding issues as the preferable way to stem the rising barbarism. He was not tempted by the appeasement of Hitler's voracious appetite.

The diary reveals a philosopher of culture who knew that the world of meaning was constructed by humanity. Museums, music, art, churches, dance, food, wine, all received his careful perusal. The diary shows the man acting, thinking, absorbing, and striving to understand. The philosopher of nature is also found in the pages of the journal, as he meditated upon forests, landscapes, mountains, and seas. The pages testify to the integrity of the thinking person, a person who lived his philosophy.

Church and Society

Tillich traveled to Europe again in 1937 for the Oxford Conference on Life and Work, sponsored by the ecumenical church and society movement. He played a leading role at the conference, where he saw many of his conceptions from religious socialism become important to ecumenical Christian social thought. He felt that he made some impact on the ecumenical movement by helping it to recognize that God often speaks to the churches through those who work for social justice even if they are not Christian. His formal contribution to the ecumenical movement was confined to this one conference, as he was bypassed when invitations were offered to postwar conferences and gatherings for ecumenical work.

His paper for this ecumenical gathering was "The Kingdom of God and History." It is a paper that reveals the Lutheran theologian working out of his Anglo-American context. He formulates a theology consistent with his religious socialism and addressed to the deterioration of the times. He provides a religious interpretation of history focusing on the Kingdom of God as a central symbol for religious socialism both on the continent and in America. Its theological themes are the same as the third volume of his *Systematic Theology* published in 1963.

First, he clarifies the basic concepts of history and the Kingdom of God. Then he explicates the theological relationship between the two. Finally, he applies this understanding to the concrete problems of the day. At the beginning, he sets out his own standpoint in history as a religious socialist who views the bourgeois epoch as coming to a close. He expects and hopes for a new civilization based on socialist principles open to the religious dimensions of existence. He uses the term "applied theology" in its American social-gospel context to describe the work in which he is engaged.

He argues that the meaning of the events of history is ultimately found only in the unification and purification of those events in a suprahistorical realization. History is not meaningful in itself, nor is it meaningful if disconnected from the events of history.

> History is the totality of remembered events, which are deter-
> mined by free human activity and are important for the life
> of human groups.[15]

The Kingdom of God, he says, is the unification and purification of the events of history. It is the answer to the question of the meaning of history:

> *The Kingdom of God is a symbolic expression of the ultimate meaning*
> *of existence. The social and political character of this symbol indicates*
> *a special relation between the ultimate meaning of existence and the*
> *ultimate meaning of human history.*[16]

The Kingdom of God is connected with history and makes use of the social-political categories of history, but it unifies and purifies them. It is a symbolic way of speaking of "the relationship of the unconditioned meaning of existence to actual existence."[17] The Kingdom of God expresses the ultimate victory over the demonic historical powers. History, then, is a battlefield between the power of salvation and the power of the demonic. World history is not salvation, but salvation is the meaning of world history. In history the conflict rages, but salvation is realized as demonic forces are overcome and the "final fulfillment of meaning appears."[18]

The demonic forces of the present, as discussed by Tillich, are capitalism, nationalism, and Bolshevism. All three forces are destructive of humanity and set against the Kingdom of God as the meaning of history. All three forces are driving society in the Western world to destruction. Capitalism is betraying its humanism, nationalism is betraying its reintegration of community, and Bolshevism is betraying its expectation of justice. Capitalism and nationalism had long been regarded by Tillich as demonic. The evidence of Stalin's terror now made Tillich realize the demonic quality of Bolshevism. He views the situation as truly tragic because flaws in the great movements had made them self-destructive.

This threat of the destruction of the historical epoch produces, for Tillich, a kairos. Out of the destruction could come a new church as the entanglement of Protestantism with a dying era ended.[19] Against the demonic, Christians could affirm justice against capitalism in the direction of socialism. The unity of humanity had to be affirmed against nationalism. Against Bolshevism, antidictatorial corrections in political authority had to be asserted in the symbol of human rights. Even faced with disappointment and an ongoing struggle, Tillich predicts, Christians would affirm the Kingdom of God as the answer to the question of the meaning of history, and they would struggle for social justice, universalism, and human rights.

After the conference, Tillich spent a few weeks on the continent, meeting Hannah near Mont Blanc in the Alps. His sense of the inevitability of war deepened. He left Europe, not to return until 1948.

In the summer of 1937, Tillich's essay "The Church and Communism" appeared in a series along with essays by Cornelius Krusé and Georgia E. Harkness on the church and fascism and democracy.[20] He uses the term communism, probably at the suggestion of the editor, to include all Marxist-inspired socialist parties.[21] The essay is perhaps Tillich's clearest exposition of his understanding of the relationship of Christianity to Marxism produced during the period of his prewar exile. He asserts that "the strategy of the Christian churches toward Communism has been predominantly wrong and pernicious."[22] He recommends a new strategy on the level of theory and of practice.

He pleads first that *"the churches ought to acquire an exact knowledge of Communism."*[23] This knowledge needs to include the theoretical foundations of Marxism and its development. Second, he says, the actual history of communism needs to be understood. With this knowledge, the churches could interpret communism as a *"secularized and politicized form of Christian prophetism."*[24] An interpretation from a Christian perspective could understand the religious elements within Marxism. Before criticizing Marxism, Tillich argues, the churches need to recognize the truth in Marxist criticism of capitalism and nationalism. Then the churches can criticize the secularism, the utopianism, and the political tyrannies of Marxism.

On the level of practical strategy, Tillich notes that a correct practical position depends on a correct theoretical stance. Officially, the church ought to remain neutral concerning Marxism as a political movement. It should join with Marxism in the critique of demonic aspects of society and also criticize the demonic aspects of Marxism. Ministers representing the church should observe neutrality, but in their private lives, they can involve themselves more directly. Christian lay people might become communists and try to unite communist principles with Christian principles. Christian socialism, nonetheless, ought to remain independent of the churches themselves.

> *The practical strategy of the Church as a whole is a continuous attempt to make herself a representation and anticipation of the kingdom of God and its righteousness.*[25]

The church can solve the social problem only in itself. It cannot resolve the class warfare or mass disintegration of the present; however, it can witness to the Kingdom of God and achieve community in the present. Again and again the churches will need to search for the right balance of *"religious reservation from history and religious obligation toward history."*[26]

In the United States, writing for the churches in general, Tillich made the connections between socialism and Christianity less explicit than in writing for his socialist friends in Germany. Religious socialism was an option, but not for the whole church. Also, he had just argued against Christian identification with Nazism, and he was careful to stress the Christian reservation about any political party. At the same time that he tried to teach the churches about Marxism and tried to get the churches to ally themselves with aspects of the Marxist critique, he urged them to keep religious socialism as a movement while the church remained unidentified with any political party.

For his first five years in the United States, Tillich refrained from speaking at public political rallies. On November 21, 1938, he spoke on German anti-Semitism in New York City's Madison Square Garden.[27] He asked for unity between Christians and Jews on the grounds of prophetic religion, and he appealed to German-Americans to oppose Nazism for the sake of the true meaning of Germany. He regarded Nazism's attack on Judaism as an attack upon the God of Christianity. The demons of blood, soil, race, nation, state, and culture were opposing the God of Abraham. The demons could not win, but the contest would be severe. He opposed Nazi ideology with references to the universalism of German classicism and noted the debt of Germany to Jewish contributors. He reminded the audience that Friedrich Nietzsche, whom the Nazis were trying to claim, had denounced anti-Semitism. The speech was an educated polemic, urging solidarity with the Jews and attacking the Nazis. His two worlds were on a collision course; next year would see war.

X.
World War II

The closing months of 1938 and the spring and summer of 1939 were busy months of international diplomacy. The democracies of France and England vacillated before the determined, aggressive diplomacy of Italy, Japan, and Germany. The United States remained ineffective, and the Soviet Union contemplated various security arrangements that would further its interests. In retrospect, it was a time of deciding when the war would come and who would be allies.

Located between the major powers, the weaker countries—including Finland, Estonia, Latvia, Lithuania, Poland, and Czechoslovakia—were the bargaining chips of the deadly game being played. Earlier appeasement in the Far East, Africa, and Spain had encouraged the fascists to risk belligerency. The Munich pact of September, 1938, sacrificed Czechoslovakia to Hitler and encouraged Stalin to divide Poland with Hitler the following summer. The French and English bought peace in Munich, and Russia bought peace from Ribbentrop in Moscow in August, 1939. The two pacts for peace insured that war would come.

Tillich knew that no compromise was possible with Nazism. In 1938, aware of the relativities of judgment and ambiguity of political action, he had called for a life-and-death struggle against Nazism.[1] Commenting on the Munich agreement before the outbreak of war,

Tillich isolated five factors as presuppositions of the situation: Those people operating in nineteenth-century categories of continual progress were unprepared to understand events of the twentieth century. The foreign policies of the various countries depended upon the interests of the ruling classes. The politics of leftist forces in the democracies were inept. Fascism promised an answer to the insecurities of the present. Collective security had not worked, and the Munich settlement recognizing a German protectorate over central Europe was unstable.[2]

War seemed inevitable. The encirclement policy that followed Munich was a reaction of the old empires to the new German empire. The policy depended upon Russia, and Tillich feared that dependence on Russia was foolhardy.

Several contradictory conditions in Germany were obvious to Tillich. There was a contradiction between the mass movement of Nazism and its foundation of terror. Capitalism was being both preserved and transformed. Economic problems were being resolved by a war economy, but the economy was threatened by a war conducted by a mass society. The rhetoric was of both nationalism and supranational imperialism. All these instabilities in Germany were overcome by repression.

Tillich thought in 1939 that there was still a chance that the emergence of a German empire in central Europe would be tolerated by the democracies. However, if Germany reached agreement with Russia, war would follow. He recognized that the Russian-German alliance must be prevented, but that it was probably too late to stop it, and he supported the growing toughness of Roosevelt's foreign policy.

Religious leadership, he felt, had been largely irresponsible in the face of the developing situation. In a short discussion of power and justice, he refuted religious pacifism as a possible response. Democracy to survive would have to realize internal justice and not just observe the forms of legal justice. In the twentieth century, the emptiness of meaning and the lack of justice allowed demonic totalitarianism to rush into the vacuum.

The German invasion of Poland on September 1, 1939, with the assistance of Russia, drove Tillich into a period of discouragement and despair. He had anticipated war and urged preparation for it, but the actuality of it brought back too many painful dreams and memories of his own time in the trenches of World War I. During this second world conflagration, his actions were first to become an American citizen and then to join in the public debate over the aims and policies of the war, to continue to assist refugees, to write on the war, and to join the American propaganda war after the United States was brought into the conflict.

Tillich's work among refugees had emphasized the need for a real migration. He urged Germans to identify with their new country and to free themselves from illusory hopes for a return. On March 4, 1940, he became a U.S. citizen, and in an essay celebrating his new status, he affirmed his ability as a citizen to participate in building the future.[3] Europe, for him, became identified more and more with the past. He also tried to recant certain German characteristics that seemed to be provincial in light of the worldwide migration to the United States. His great contribution, however, was to represent the best of German thought to America. His most important writings appeared in the U.S. in English, but his thought was formed before he became an American and the patterns were all established before 1940.

In 1941, Kenneth Leslie attracted Tillich to his journal *The Protestant Digest* (soon changed to *The Protestant*), and Tillich wrote several essays for it in 1941–1943. Leslie was a rather independent editor, and he was constantly in tension with his editorial board of which Paul Tillich became chairman. One of the disputes led Tillich to write a policy statement for the journal in 1942. It is one of Tillich's most succinct statements of the relationship of Christian faith to political action; it appeared under the title "Protestant Principles."[4]

> 1. Protestantism affirms the absolute majesty of
> God alone and raises prophetic protest against every
> human claim, ecclesiastical or secular, to absolute
> truth and authority.
>
> 2. Protestantism affirms the Christian message as the
> ultimate expression of the nature of the Divine and pro-

tests against all attempts to dissolve this message
into a complex of religious experiences, moral demands
and philosophical doctrines.

3. Protestantism affirms Divine sovereignty over the
institutions and doctrines of the Christian churches and
protests against attempts to bind the Christian
message to the life and law of any historical Church.

4. Protestantism affirms the direct reference of
the Divine to every element of reality and protests
against hierarchical mediations as well as against
the separation of a sacred from a secular realm.

5. Protestantism affirms the independent structure
of the different spheres of the cultural life and
protests against encroachments upon their autonomy
by churches and states.

6. Protestantism affirms the dependence of the
spiritual meaning of all cultural activities on their
religious foundation and protests against the
separation of religious transcendence from cultural
immanence.

7. Protestantism, while rejecting any definitive
or final system of Christian ethics and politics,
applies the Christian message to every historical
situation as the principle of criticism and demand.

In a following issue of the journal, Tillich commented on the
principles in response to readers reactions.[5] He set out his belief that
the essence of Protestantism, or prophetic religion, is the dual recognition of the transcendence and immanence of God. All of life has
a religious base, but life itself is not divine. Religion has two senses:
its special proclamation of its vision of God and the denial that its
special proclamation is absolute. All of life points toward its source,
but the source is not captured by any expression of life. Vital religion
announces the "end of religion" in the sense of criticising the absolute pretensions of religious communities, but vital religion continues to affirm the human need for religious symbols to express the
ultimate.

This dialectical approach conditions Protestantism's relationship to both the church and the world. Both are affirmed, both are criticized. Therefore, in politics there is no absolute Christian answer, but continual Christian enjoyment in the pursuit of answers. "Protestantism is not bound to its past; therefore it is free for its future, even if this future should deserve the name: 'Post Protestant Era.' "[6]

Tillich's first statement regarding appropriate war aims had appeared in 1941 in *The Protestant Digest*. He blamed the democracies for creating communism by nurturing social injustice and of having used fascism to combat communism. The war was a struggle by fascism to destroy the humanism of the West, he argued, and the appropriate war aim should be the creation of a planned economy in a European federal union, which could be liberal enough to prevent tyranny while assuring economic security to the masses of Europe. Liberal arbitrariness could be overcome without sacrificing freedom, he thought, and nationalism reduced by an economic federation. The war aims that appeared in serial form in the journal were brought together as a pamphlet and sold for a nickel to contribute to the American discussion of goals of the war.[7]

Eventually the sponsors of the journal differed over the editorial position regarding communism. *The Protestant* folded as a result of the dispute, and Leslie, who was too close to communism for many on the board, returned to his native Canada. The split among the sponsors of the journal was symptomatic of what happened to many of Tillich's projects in the war period and, beyond that, foreshadowed the tensions that would divide the victors of World War II and result in the cold war.

Anti-Semitism

The relationship among Jews, Germans, and Christians was a central problem for Tillich. Many of his associates in the Institute for Social Research were Jewish as were many of his other dearest friends. When he had been asked to deliver the Founders' Day address at the University of Frankfurt a few days before Hitler came to power, he stressed the Jewish contribution to German culture from Spinoza to Marx.[8] His defense of Jewish students contributed to his dismissal from the university. His first public speech in America against the regime in Germany dealt with its anti-Semitism. Therefore, when someone in the Office of War Information asked Tillich to prepare a series of lectures for broadcast into Germany over the Voice of America, it was not surprising that his first address was on "The Jewish Question." This first talk was broadcast on March 31, 1942. It was followed by weekly messages, written by Tillich but read by an official of the Voice of America, and broadcast on Sundays through September 5, 1944.

Each lecture was addressed to *Meine deutschen Freunde* (my German friends). He spoke in the first talk primarily to Protestant churchpeople, identifying himself as a theologian and philosopher of history.[9] The religion of Protestant Christians, he said, is of Jewish origin, and the Christian God of Jewish descent. The Old Testament is part of the Christian Bible, and the Reformation was founded in the spirit and name of this Jewish Paul. Christians cannot surrender their Jewish origins without giving up their Christianity. He noted that those who attacked Judaism were giving up their Christianity, and he called on Christians to defend Jews resolutely.

He reiterated the theme of *The Socialist Decision,* that Judaism possessed the vocation of witnessing to the just God of time over against the gods of space. As long as there is history, Tillich said, as had Paul, there will be Jews witnessing to the God of history. If world history has meaning, then the Jewish question must be seen in the context of that meaning.

He referred to the theories of the persecution of the Jews as a minority or as a different religious group, but he asserted that the basis of the Jewish question rested in the vocation of the Jews in history. The prophets had resisted and relativized nationalism; now a resurgent nationalism was taking revenge. The German people were guilty for acquiescing in the terror and for failing to offer the resistance that was possible. The defense of Judaism was the defense of the meaning of humanity against a demonic nationalism. The persecution of the Jewish people was not only human misery and shame for every German, but it was blasphemy and opposition to God.[10] The persecution of the Jews raised ultimately a question of salvation or judgment.

During the war Tillich prepared two manuscripts on anti-Semitism.[11] In his 1953 lectures on "The Jewish Question" in Berlin, he
drew upon some of the material in these papers, which were each
twenty-one pages in length and seemed to be background papers
written for a non-theologically educated audience. They possess
characteristics that point toward a wartime government use; perhaps
someone in the Office of War Information, which used so many
German intellectuals, including Thomas Mann, asked Tillich to do
these studies.

The important distinction that Tillich drew was between historical Christian anti-Judaism and racial anti-Semitism. Christianity as a
Jewish renewal movement contained polemical anti-Judaism writings in its sacred scriptures. Anti-Semitism, on the other hand, with
its racial emphasis, "is never used officially by the Church."[12] The
term anti-Semitism was a recent term evolving about 1880 and
having its origins in England and France as well as Germany.

Tillich traced anti-Judaism from the New Testament, through the
church fathers, to the position of Innocent III and the Fourth Lateran
Council. Innocent III's letter of 1199 couples a rejection of Judaism
with protection of Jews. Tillich summarized: "Seclusion and protection: This is the Catholic attitude of Anti-Judaism. Eradication: This
is the Fascist attitude of Anti-Semitism."[13] Tillich also noted how, on
the grounds of Catholic anti-Judaism, an anti-Semitism could arise as
it did in France in the Dreyfus affair and later in Vichy France in
1940. In America, Father Coughlin's anti-Semitism was tolerated by
the church for too long before he was finally silenced. In practice,
Catholic anti-Judaism could evolve into anti-Semitism, but in theory,
anti-Semitism was not the position of the church. Catholic rejection
of religious toleration made it impossible to expect the elimination
of anti-Judaism, but anti-Semitism could be fought within the framework of Catholic thought.

In his paper on "Protestantism and Anti-Semitism," Tillich commented on a collection of official Protestant statements made in
America and collected by M. Porter. The official statements went a
long way in condemning anti-Semitism. Tillich regarded as the most
profound the statement in 1938 by the Greater New York Federation of Churches, for it recognized the inner tendency of Christians

to practice "the sin of anti-Semitism." Tillich believed that Christendom nurtured anti-Judaism. The sectarian movements of Protestantism, by encouraging religious toleration, attacked anti-Judaism, but there were still problems because of the anti-Judaism in Christian scriptures. Tillich pointed out that official condemnation of anti-Semitism, though praiseworthy, did not guarantee the removal of anti-Semitism from local Protestant congregations. The Protestants lacked the hierarchical organization of Catholicism, which could insist that church policy be carried out locally.

Tillich mentioned that his ministerial family background had bred anti-Judaic tendencies in his own mind, especially during Holy Week, but that while anti-Semitism had been discussed, it had been rejected in his father's household.

Tillich also mentioned in the paper that in the Theological Discussion Group in which he participated a great percentage of theologians rejected any aggressive attempts to convert Jews to Christianity. His own attitude was to maintain vigorous dialogue with Jews about theological issues, practical cooperation in the struggle for justice, and a willingness to assist Jews who were alienated from their Jewish roots to embrace Christianity. He affirmed the necessity of preserving Judaism to guard against a Christian relapse into paganism.[14]

In conclusion, Tillich warned that liberal Protestantism's drift to a tolerant Christian humanism might be an ambiguous gift to Judaism. If Christianity became too weakened, anti-Semitic paganism could arise as it had in Germany. In fact, he warned in his final sentence that there were signs of anti-Semitism rising in the U.S. Army.[15]

These wartime writings represent Tillich's developed thought on Judaism. After the war, he would turn to the related issues of German guilt and Zionism.

Throughout the war Tillich continued to write interpretations of political theology for the Voice of America propaganda broadcasts into Europe. They were often words of sober realism:

> Those who must speak to the enemy (as I myself have done by radio for the hundredth time this week) realize that

on the political plane they cannot say *one* word of real promise.[16]

Niebuhr was writing along similar lines during the war. Both of these Union Theological Seminary professors were commenting weekly on the world situation from a position best represented by the term "Christian realism." Niebuhr's writings had more of an Anglo-Saxon confidence in democracy and pragmatism than Tillich's. Tillich retained more of his Marxist-socialist heritage. Niebuhr's grasp of the practice of American politics and foreign policy was deeper, but Tillich more consistently plumbed the theological depths.

If the collection of Tillich's addresses possesses one common theme it is: "My German friends, in your necessary losing of this war you will find a chance to save your soul." The genius of the talks is in the consistent way in which war policy is related to economic expression of domestic policy, which in turn, rests upon the social health of a nation. The talks that are topical in nature reflect the complete social philosophy of the thinker.[17]

A Just and Durable Peace

One of the most creative responses of organized American Protestantism to the war was the work of the Federal Council of Churches' Commission on a Just and Durable Peace. Under the chairmanship of John Foster Dulles, the commission developed a philosophy of international relations and sponsored educational work in the churches on this complex subject. Dulles's moralism and his natural tendency as a lawyer toward legalism pervaded the commission's philosophy. The program of the commission was a program of those who expected to be victors in the war and who wanted to assume the responsibilities of power in creating a new order. It was very effective in lobbying for the replacement of the League of Nations with a stronger organization—what would become the United Nations.

The commission knew when it invited Tillich to deliver a series of lectures that his perspective of German religious socialism would be different. However, the gap between the commission's inclination toward a Calvinist legalism and the Lutheran theologian's dynamism was greater than Dulles anticipated.

Under the theme of the "Christian Basis of a Just and Durable Peace," Tillich delivered three addresses.[18] The first lecture interpreted the war as a world revolution and developed Tillich's theological perspective on international politics. He avoided both crusade and pacifist interpretations of Christianity, but he criticized the concepts central to the commission's ideas of "just" and "durable." Tillich's dynamism—inherited from Jacob Böhme, Luther, and Schelling—made it impossible for him to regard any imposed peace as either just or durable. In fact in his interpretation of the world revolution, he felt the grounds for World War III were already being laid.

In the second lecture, Tillich revealed his fears that after the war, the Leviathan of an uncaring, monopolistic capitalism would be enforced on Europe. Capitalism in control of technology would foster the very dehumanization process that nurtured Nazism. He saw a minor hope in the possibility of progressive elements (meaning the British Labour party, the central European underground forces, American New Deal proponents, and strong sections of the churches) cooperating with Russia for an alternative order; but his fears of Russia negated that hope. His greatest hope was that nations would achieve liberated state capitalism in which the "chaotic insecurity of monopolism is excluded" and in which individuals could participate creatively in production.

His final lecture dealt with the idea of a world order and the reality of competing nation-states. He certainly reflected no trust in balance-of-power politics, but the overcoming of nineteenth-century diplomacy by transformation to a new order was in the future. He could not visualize a center for an emerging world federation. A new order would require transforming the present technical-rationalistic manipulations of the human world into a new political-spiritual reality. In a very direct sense, Tillich called the work of the Dulles commission superficial. He expressed his fears that Europe would be reduced to a colonial hinterland of the emerging super-powers. Never spoken, but underlying his words, was his concern about the fate of the villages in which he had grown to maturity. It was in the spirit of prophetic religion, he claimed in his conclusion, that he destroyed the moralism of the Commission on a Just and Durable Peace. The theological terms of grace and tragedy, he said, were more adequate categories than the moralistic principles of the Commission to describe the present broken order.

Council for a Democratic Germany

Paul Tillich served as chairman of the Council for a Democratic Germany, a group of anti-Nazi German refugees. The council published its founding philosophy, "A Program for a Democratic Germany," in *Christianity and Crisis* in May of 1944, just before the D-Day invasion of June 6.[19] Though no author's name appears, the document was written by Tillich and represents political thought identical to that expressed elsewhere under his own name. Signers of the declaration included professors, ministers, businesspeople, politicians, actors, and writers, many of whose names are well known today. Also among the signers were those who had contact with the German underground resistance. American supporters of the statement included John C. Bennett, Norman Cousins, John Dewey, Harry Emerson Fosdick, Rufus M. Jones, Reinhold Niebuhr, William Scarlett, Dorothy Thompson, and Jonah B. Wise.

The statement presupposed that cooperation between the West and Russia was a necessary precondition for the reconstruction of Europe. Many of the signers, including the author, however, knew that such cooperation was only a precarious possibility. There were four major emphases.

Germany was part of the European problem. The defeat of Nazism and the liquidation of the Nazis were prerequisites to any solution of the problem. Also, those who supported the Nazis had to be deprived of political power. Though it assumed a disarmed Germany, the statement warned against a dismembered Germany, fearing irredentism.

The economic power of Germany should be conserved to avoid widespread poverty and future unrest. The German economic system had to be integrated with the rest of Europe to reduce the danger of German economic hegemony and rearmament.

The democratic forces in Germany must be allowed to assert

themselves and encouraged to carry out the program of denazification. The vestiges of Nazism had to be expurgated from all aspects of life by the Germans themselves.

The education of the German people had to be carried out by Germans in a context that provided security and democracy. Nazism and its spurious idea of Germany must be removed from schools, universities, books, libraries, and other cultural media. Historical experience was the primary teacher, and the imposition of American education on Germans, particularly in the absence of social justice, would be folly.

The document pleaded, as Tillich emphasized everywhere, for Americans to recognize and nurture healthy elements in German society so that the evil elements could be removed without creating a vacuum into which new evil forces would move.

The brief life of the council, 1944–1945, was characterized by internal divisions, and the refugees were unable to agree upon policy for postwar Germany. The council's basic opposition to extreme measures of punishment for Germany was criticized, and for a short time, Tillich was blacklisted by the U.S. Army. Eventually, the tensions represented in the developing cold war drained the council of its life, and it expired. What policy it had depended on a united Germany and some cooperation between the U.S. and the U.S.S.R. With division and antagonism, it had no program. In later years when Tillich would refuse to participate in some political activities, he would point to his chairmanship of the council and attribute his withdrawal from active politics to its failure.

He had actually argued for a theology of liberation: the liberation of Europe by the Allied armies and the equipping of Germans for self-liberation in a Nazi-free Germany. With the imposition of military rule and the return of monopoly capitalism after the war, Tillich's dream of a liberating religious socialism had almost no chance for realization.

"The World Situation"

Since 1934 Tillich had met semiannually with a body that called itself the Theological Discussion Group. The gathering included the Niebuhr brothers, Roland Bainton, Robert Calhoun, John Bennett,

Henry P. Van Dusen, Douglas Steere, George F. Thomas, John Mackay, Georgia Harkness, Benjamin Mays, John Knox, Theodore M. Greene, Samuel McCrea Cavert, Edwin E. Aubrey, Wilhelm Pauck, and others. Originally a young gathering, the group gradually came to represent something of an establishment in American theology. Its members considered the group an important channel of cross-fertilization of ideas. The meetings were generally informal and consisted of discussions of scholarly papers.

Henry Van Dusen sensed an emerging consensus among the group, and in 1945 he edited a collection of essays by its members entitled *The Christian Answer*. [21] Tillich contributed the lead piece, "The World Situation." This essay represents Tillich's most complete social analysis of the late war years. The outcome of the war was clear by the time he wrote in 1944, but the atomic bomb and the overt split between Russia and the U.S. were not yet in evidence.

Though Van Dusen's introduction to the volume emphasizes the original process by which the essays were written, criticized, and rewritten, the content of Tillich's essay is not really new. Much of the argument is from *The Religious Situation,* which had been published in Germany in 1926, and other material is from a manuscript that remained in fragment form. Tillich had begun work on a volume on "Religion and World Politics," which was to be published in German by a Dutch publishing firm. The outbreak of the war ended that project, but much of the conceptual argument appears in "The World Situation" and the original fragment is available in German. [22] Some of Tillich's characteristic dialectic disappeared under Van Dusen's editing, and the claims for the ecumenical church sometimes seem to owe more to Van Dusen than to Tillich. However, the essay, which has been reprinted for popular distribution, [23] remains one of Tillich's most important statements on social philosophy from his American writings.

The work is an attempt by a Westerner to discover the meaning of a revolution that is absorbing the whole world. The determining fact of the emerging, interconnected world is seen as the bourgeois triumph over feudalism and subsequent control over the fate of the world and, most importantly, the ensuing revolt against bourgeois life. World War II is presented as the absorption of the world in the struggle of forces arising out of the failure of bourgeois society to provide security and meaning.

In monopoly capitalism armed with technology, humanity had created a Leviathan that was nearly irresistible. The chaos of bourgeois economic life and the wars of the twentieth century, says Tillich, refute the myth of laissez-faire harmony, and society is now in revolt against liberal capitalism. In Italy and Germany it is a fascist revolt; in the U.S. and England it takes the form of New Deal planning and mild socialist measures; and in Russia, communism expresses the revolt. Humanity could not return to the capitalism of recurrent depressions, Tillich argues, so planning is inevitable. Tillich, however, hopes for an order that will avoid "totalitarian absolutism" and "liberal individualism." The danger he sees ahead is the modern Leviathan, totalitarianism.

In "The World Situation," Tillich shows how personality and community evolve together. His analysis ranges over art, family structure, and education, revealing that the political-economic substance of a culture dominates these cultural expressions. Politics and economics are interdependent, he says, and cannot be separated. Much of postwar Christian social ethics would have had more depth if this interdependence of economics and politics had been kept in view.

Throughout the essay, Tillich's concern for structures that would protect the masses from economic insecurity emerges. His own early experience among the workers in Berlin after the First World War inclines his writing in favor of security for the masses, and he calls for breaking the power of "large vested interests."[24] Christianity, he argues, must be committed in its struggle against dehumanization to an alliance with the masses for economic reorganization of the system.

Tillich was not an absolutist in defense of democracy as a constitutional form of government. He thought that liberal democracy demanded prerequisites that were not present in most of the world. The basic principle of his political ethics was the rendering of justice to the "dignity of every human being."[25] A distinction must be made, he argued, between the constitutional system of democracy and democracy as the protection of human dignity. Christianity was allied to the latter cause, but not necessarily to any political form. His colleague Reinhold Niebuhr wrote *The Children of Light and the Children of Darkness* at about this same time. As an American with a different experience of democracy, Niebuhr offered a more thoroughgoing defense of democracy. The two were very close in politics, but Niebuhr was more of a radical democrat than Tillich and, after the war, more prone than Tillich to a cold-war defense of democracy. Christianity for Tillich could not sanction forms of democracy that hid the "destruction of community and personality."[26]

The old balance of power politics of nineteenth-century Europe was inadequate for the twentieth century. Tillich saw hope resting in a federation of nations not overly dominated by the victorious allies, but the world lacked the unifying spirit to make such a federation a reality. Christianity had to commit itself to the building of a common spirit within the world. Such a task required an inclusive, ecumenical Christianity. Existential and universal truth would need to be unified within an inclusive church if the church were to rise to the occasion demanded by the world situation.

He summarized the situation: A world revolution was under way against a decaying bourgeois order. Christianity had to protect the masses from meaninglessness and insecurity by promoting a new order. Such an agenda required an ecumenical, progressive Christianity, which remained realistic in the midst of tragedy and eschewed utopian solutions. Tillich's vision during the closing years of the war was essentially the same as during the years of the Wiemar Republic. The victory of an autonomous humanity was affirmed in all its radicalness. Solutions of returning to totalitarian heteronomy were to be avoided even when autonomy was threatening, but humanity had to move on to a theonomous culture in which a modern solution for people in community could be found.

Across the street from the Union Seminary Tower in which Tillich wrote his philosophy, another group was working on the atomic bomb. The headquarters of the Manhattan Project, located on the campus of Columbia University, was visible from Union. The detonation of the world's first two atomic bombs on Japan would end the war, but plunge humanity into a new, revolutionary, world situation.

XI.
Social Ethics in America

Tillich was deeply disappointed that his work on behalf of a program of democratic-socialist reconstruction of Germany was ignored. His one attempt to influence President Roosevelt toward the program of the Council for a Democratic Germany was a failure. Roosevelt rebuffed Tillich's ideas of moderation, insisted on the destruction of Germany, and suggested that the professors confine themselves to writing textbooks for a conquered Germany.[1] In ecclesiastical circles the moralism of the Dulles Commission on a Just and Durable Peace prevailed, and the Council for a Democratic Germany folded under the pressure of cold-war issues.

The war ended; fifty million were dead. The European world a disaster area morally, economically, culturally, spiritually, and politically. Tillich's native provinces were occupied by the Russians and destined to become part of Poland. Tillich worked hard to secure food, clothing, and other necessities for war-ravaged Germans, and in 1948, he returned to occupied Germany and viewed first hand the suffering war had brought. It was clear that the security and well-being of the German people were in the hands of their conquerors and would be determined by the world situation rather than by German initiative. The people, in shock and confusion, were finding some center in their religious traditions, but Tillich could not rejoice in the social-cultural direction of either postwar Catholicism or Protestantism.

Now was not a time of kairos as was the period after the First World War; it was a time of totalitarian tendencies obscured by democracy. It was a time characterized by conformity, resignation, and mysticism, with very little cultural creativity. Tillich saw the world split in a demonic division between the West and the Soviet Union. If, with hindsight, his political projections in the twenties and early thirties can be regarded as too romantic, his projections of the forties, fifties, and early sixties may be thought of by some people as overly pessimistic. But at the end of the seventies we still have not reaped the fruits of postwar world politics, so we lack a perspective from which to refute him. His judgment that American society was characterized more by continuity than by radical change seems justified.

After the war Tillich's work in social thought became less directly political than it had been in the Wiemar Republic. During the war, his involvement with political issues had been high as a refugee from the enemy government and as a spokesman for an alternative Germany. Following the war, his writing on society focused more on social ethical issues and less on politics. Particularly, he displayed only a moderate interest in American politics. His religious-socialist vision was grounded in German interwar politics and was alien to the times of postwar American politics. Of course, judgment is relative to the perspective one takes on Tillich. If he is regarded as a theologian, his numerous speeches on social philosophy and his writings on issues of political philosophy are quite remarkable. Compared to his role in Frankfurt as a professor of philosophy lecturing on social philosophy, among other topics, his involvement in political issues in the U.S. after the war is minimal.

Three factors combined to influence Tillich to become less involved in politics. First, his political mentors Reinhold Niebuhr and John C. Bennett shifted away from their socialist persuasion and influenced Tillich to regard his religious socialism as relatively nonapplicable to the American situation. Tillich relied heavily upon both of them, as well as on James Luther Adams, for practical guidance to American politics. Second, Tillich emphasized the psychological aspects of the human condition. He felt it imperative to relate psychological insights to the Christian understanding of human nature. In so doing he fought against the pressures in mass-culture America to force people to conform to a narrow, middle-class view of life. His socialist critique was still operating, but few understood the deep political nature of the enterprise.

> And the relation of theology to psychotherapy became a more urgent problem than the relation of the Christian message to the social and international order. The paralyzing "cold war" contributed to this temporary turning away from the political sphere. But the main cause, as theologians saw it, was the need to rethink the Christian doctrine of man in the light of the enormous material brought forth by the psychoanalytic methods and theories.[2]

Finally, he made a vocational choice to complete the *Systematic Theology,* which events had delayed so long. Even in this work, however, the political dimension emerges in the shape of the basic vision of the Kingdom of God.[3] The factors that influenced him away from direct political participation resulted in his social thought being most fully presented in his writings on social ethics, in some practical involvements, and in his *Systematic Theology.*

Christian Social Ethics

The breakdown of the great Hegelian synthesis in the hands of Schelling, Nietzsche, Feuerbach, Freud, and Marx convinced Tillich that human thought is never complete. He found this lack of completeness particularly to be the case in Christian ethics. He learned a great deal from Ernst Troeltsch about the historical relativity of Christian ethical judgments. Tillich began a 1962 lecture in Dallas with the assertion that there was not any one accepted system of Christian ethics. The whole direction of his thought inclined him to the conclusion that there would never be a final, authoritative system of Christian ethics. In World War I, he experienced the irrelevance of the ethics he had inherited as a Lutheran. In the German revolution of 1918, he experienced the ideological misapplication of his beloved Lutheran tradition as most of the Lutheran church forces lined up on the side of social reaction. Though religious socialism became for him a working social ethic, he always kept it in a tentative position by his loyalty to the essence of the Reformation. That essence, which he described as the "Protestant principle," was the stubborn insistence that no moral practice or ethical system could take the place of the absolute. The dual love commandment of Jesus expressed the Protestant principle and, though itself absolute, was not law in any ordinary sense. Rather, it was a summary of Christian ethics, the meaning of which was not immediately obvious for most ethical situations. The Christian ethic was always in the process of being worked out, and Tillich plunged into the fray of ethical debate with his usual vigor.

Two recent essays on Tillich's ethics have labeled his method as an "ontological self-realization ethic"[4] and as "metaphysical ethics."[5] Now, it is true that nearly everything Tillich wrote can be related to his constructive ontology, but it is not true that his ethic was deduced from his ontology. His ethic is more complicated in form than the labeling of it as a metaphysical ethic permits. In *Das System der Wissenschaften* (*The System of Sciences*, 1923), he distinguished ethics from metaphysics, the social sciences, and theology.

Ethics as a discipline cannot be known in itself, he said. It only becomes an object of knowledge when it is placed in a frame of reference. The necessary frame of reference for Tillich was a system, and the role of ethics in his mind when he wrote more about it in his later years was consistent with the place he gave it in *The System of Sciences*. In this ambitious undertaking, he dared to satisfy his mind by attempting to perceive the unity of all the sciences. Ethics was conceived of as belonging to the mental sciences, distinguished from the sciences of being and the sciences of thought, and could not be reduced to logic or empirical studies. His tripartite division of the sciences was also expressed as the sciences of form, or ideal science, the sciences of objects, or real science, and the sciences of norms, or normative science.

Tillich considered the subsuming of ethics in theories of sociology to have weakened the understanding of ethics as the active direction toward the unconditional. Destruction of the ethos reduced ethics to morality, that is, the theory of compulsory behavior in the context of the conditional. The dignity of ethics could be preserved by understanding it as the science of the ethos, that is, the understanding of practical activity moving toward the realization of the unconditional. Therefore, the place of ethics in the practical realm was analogous to that of metaphysics in the theoretical realm. Tillich was concerned to maintain the autonomy of the social sciences. Sociological analysis had its own dignity and independence, even though the content expressed in its forms is determined by ethical attitudes. Ethics, as the science of the ethos, expresses itself in transcendent symbols and knows that its unconditional communities are not to be realized concretely. Ethics can analyze the content of community apart from any particular realization of community.

The social sciences have exploded in their development since Tillich's organization of his work on the sciences. It is a safe projection, however, to see his attitude as one that used all the social sciences in their formal understanding, but insisted that the content of their goals came from ethics, which was understood as the direction of practical activity toward the unconditional.

Ethics, then, was manifested in philosophy or ontology, in intellectual history, and in its own role as the normative system of the goals of the community. Tillich was concerned to protect the relative autonomy of ethics while placing it in a larger scheme of meaning, but it definitely was neither theology nor metaphysics to him.

Tillich shared in the movement of vitalism, expressed differently by Schelling, Nietzsche, and Bergson. Ethics was not to be reduced to a morality that confined, but was to reveal the way to fulfillment of the self in the community. The normative science of the self and the community was directed toward the divine meaning of the self and the community. Within the ambiguities of life and the struggle of various beings to fulfill life, that which was moral was the act in which the potential to be a person was realized.[6] Recognition of the drive for fulfillment of the self in the community gave his thought a radical direction in terms of both personal morality and social morality. This recurring motif in his writing on ethics could lead to the conclusion that his was a teleological or goal-oriented ethic, but there are deontological or rule elements present also. The model of beings struggling for the fulfillment of their power to be gave his ethic a realism, but he also saw that it was in the struggle that the need for justice was found. The encounter of person with person demanded justice, that is, an arrangement that would allow both to become what they could. Similarly, among classes and nations the need for justice arose so that all could find fulfillment in relationship with one another. As a follower of Troeltsch, Tillich knew that Christian ethical judgments had changed through the centuries on almost every issue. As he sought for an absolute amidst relativity, he could find only one: the commandment to love the neighbor as the self. This commandment, grounded in the first commandment, of course, contained within itself the requirements of justice and the need for wisdom. Love, justice, and wisdom, then, were the norms that worked together in a properly ethical decision.

Tillich's ethic reflects his life, and an adequate treatment of his ethic must take account of the experiences that broke open his life. The experience of World War I shattered his political complacency and his Lutheran conservatism. The seduction of his first wife by a friend while he was at the front shattered his conventional sexual morality. His experiences among the workers and the revolution in Germany shattered his aristocratic tendencies. The disaster of Nazism destroyed his German academic community, and the occupation of his homeland by the Russians after World War II made permanent his exile. Temperamentally, he was inclined to a philosophical idealism, but the destruction of so many of the foundations of his life tore him from his roots, and only his belief kept him a faithful realist rather than a cynic. This faithful realism is perhaps best expressed philosophically in *Love, Power, and Justice.*

Elements of his Lutheran heritage remained even after all the shocks. His ethic retained a provisional dualism, distinguishing between the moral expectations appropriate of groups and of individuals. He was never attracted to the Christian pacifism of many American social activists, and his social realism owes much to his Lutheran heritage. On the other hand, his socialism and concern for social justice on theological grounds set him apart from the conservative Brandenburg Lutheranism in which he grew up.

Paul Tillich, like all people of courage, was also subject to fears. Late in life at the height of his professional success, he did not emphasize the full radicalness of his earlier Christian Marxism. On occasion, he would suppress the republication of a socialist piece that he felt was irrelevant to the present and potentially dangerous to his career. However, he never denied his earlier socialism and often explicitly defended it before conservative audiences.

In the realm of personal ethics, he hinted in his lectures that he was exploring new paths of personal fulfillment. He explicitly attacked conventional morality. He regarded divorce as a possible demand of agape. He dealt publicly with the idea of sexual relations with partners other than the marriage partner, and he discussed the possessive sexual jealousy that undercuts relationships.[7] In this realm, however, Tillich only hinted at the radicalness of his life, and it took the publication of his wife's memoirs to reveal the meaning of the clues found in his lectures. It should be stated, also, that he often commented on how difficult it was to discuss sexual problems nonlegalistically. He acknowledged the incompleteness and failure of both his theory and practice in the realms of politics and sexuality. It is best to regard him as a man who defied convention and who paid the price of that risk in loneliness and suffering. The price was one that he mentioned as the cost of the search for unconventional patterns of life.

His boldest move in theoretical ethics was an essay entitled "The Transmoral Conscience."[8] He analyzed the meaning of conscience in scripture and philosophy and found the transcendence of the conscience in Nietzsche and Heidegger dangerous. His own tentative formulation of the transmoral conscience was grounded in Luther's idea of justification by faith and not by the correspondence of an act to conscience. He concluded that any sensitive conscience will be an uneasy conscience. Transmoral could mean either the claim of morality beyond moral law or the destruction of morality. Tillich's conclusions affirmed transmoral conscience in the former sense, that is, the conscience that acted creatively for justice even while setting aside accepted canons of justice.

Despite the complexity of the biographical formulation of Tillich's ethic and the wide range of sources from which it is drawn, the form of his ethic is clear and consistent. The structure is threefold:

first, the ultimate principle of Christian ethics is agape, which is known as the law of human nature; the second part of the structure is human wisdom as represented in laws, moral principles, and guidelines; third is the concrete situation in which the actor takes upon himself the risk of moral decision. This pattern of love, law, and situation is present in most of Tillich's writing on ethics.

Agape is the one universal element of the human moral situation in Tillich's view. Occasionally, he describes the universal element as "the human itself." The seeming ambivalence in his ethics, of course, derives from his claim that a properly conducted analysis of human nature reveals love as the essence of life. In much of his writing, however, it seems that the experience of love is the starting point of the analysis: "In man's experience of love the nature of life becomes manifest."[9]

The second level of the theory accepts the relativity of all moral principles unless they are alternative formulations of agape, which in itself includes justice and the honoring of a person as a person. Moral principles, or middle axioms, are not despised, but they are considered thoroughly relative. They are useful as guidelines, and if they embody agape and meet the situation, they may be the ground upon which the moral decision-maker acts.

The third ingredient—the situation—requires a loving receptiveness on the part of the decision-maker. It is at this point that the tools of the social and psychological sciences have their greatest importance for Tillich. His antimoralism demands that as many of the particulars of the situation as possible be understood.

In Tillich's ethic, there is no security; there is only the risk of moral decision and the comfort that trust in the power of forgiveness brings.

Justice

Justice was not a central term of Paul Tillich's religious-socialist polemic against capitalism. He did not judge capitalism by the criterion of justice; rather, he assumed that the contradictions within capitalism were fatal. Because he regarded the spirit of capitalism as the proclamation of a self-sufficient finitude, his basic argument with it was that it was not open to the experience of the unconditional.[10]

Capitalism encouraged competition, alienation, and meaninglessness, and it was self-destructive.

Justice became a central concept for Tillich in his American experience at a period when the socialist cause, or at least the expression of it in the categories of the young Marx, seemed irrelevant to the social scene. Two exceptions to this generalization are his essays "Grundlinien des Religiösen Sozialismus" (1923)[11] and "Man and Society in Religious Socialism" (1943).[12] Neither essay discusses justice in the ontological depths of his later work or uses justice as a weapon with which to criticize society the way Reinhold Niebuhr did in the same period. It could be said, also, that his Hegelian background is just below the surface in the 1923 work, and the 1943 essay is more reminiscent of the political philosophical discussions in England and America.

Human nature, according to the latter essay, makes the claim that every human being be recognized as person.[13] There is a natural equality, which is the equality of claim to express one's creativity (later he would say "power of being"): "This is the ultimate criterion of justice."[14] Justice concedes to finitude that the contingent characteristics of human existence prevent absolute equality. But justice requires that accidental, or existential, differences—by which he meant sex, race, intelligence, strength, class—ought not infringe upon essential equality. Therefore, all the structures that reinforce *essential* inequality are to be opposed. Fascism, monopolistic capitalism, class-determined education, all result in dehumanization, or the violation of the opportunity to express one's power of being; and, therefore, they are enemies of justice.

Tillich's 1954 work *Love, Power, and Justice* is his most systematic discussion of justice. Here, as the title suggests, he unites reflection on justice to two concepts on which he had worked for years, love and power. He attempts to find a way between realists, who would reduce justice to the meaning of power, and idealists, who would assert the demands of justice without reference to power. He seeks to overcome the dichotomy in Protestant ethics between justice and love without collapsing them into each other.

Tillich's discussion of the method of the volume is confusing.[15] The method is that of conceptual analysis of the basic categories of ethics and politics. Tillich asserts that such elaboration is the work of ontology. Consequently, he calls conceptual analysis of terms that have ontological implications as well as other meanings, ontological analysis. Much of his method is etymology, a search for root meanings of terms, but Tillich also regards this search as ontological. Thus, a reading of Tillich's argument leads to the conclusion that the relationship of love, power, and justice is but one model reflecting several human, even political, decisions, rather than a relationship necessarily rooted in the way things ultimately are. Tillich's Protestant principle forces him to agree with the above conclusion.

"Justice is the form in which the power of being actualizes itself, . . ."[16] In Tillich's ontology all beings drive toward transcending themselves. This drive produces competition, and justice is the form that allows creativity to be expressed without destroying the whole. Every act of justice is an act at the third level of ethics, that is, an existential act with the risk of decision. However, there are universal principles of justice that are contained within the first level of ethical analysis.

At the center of the principles of justice is love that contains adequacy, equality, personality, and liberty. Tillich rejected community or fraternity as part of the formal definition of justice, but his rejection seems to slight the importance of the issue. Community is certainly more than "an emotional principle adding nothing essential to the rational concept of justice."[17] All through the discussion of the principles of justice, Tillich can be seen analyzing the concepts as they appeared historically, but also stipulating his preferred meanings. The stipulations reflect his religious-socialist background and his protest against dehumanization.

The principles of justice are applied at various levels. He lists the intrinsic; the tributive, including distributive, attributive, and retributive; and the transforming. Tillich's discussion of the transforming level of justice reveals most clearly the biblical roots of his concept of justice. Transforming or creative justice is the form of love that does what is necessary for the reunion of beings.

> Love does not do more than justice demands, but love is the ultimate principle of justice. Love reunites; justice preserves

what is to be united. It is the form in which and through which love performs its work. Justice in its ultimate meaning is creative justice, and creative justice is the form of reuniting love.[18]

The influence of Hegel is strong in *Love, Power, and Justice,* and the fragment on love is particularly influential. Tillich's oft-repeated statement that the relationship between theology and politics is the driving force of Hegel's system applies only a little less accurately to Tillich himself and particularly to the Tillich of *Love, Power, and Justice.*

Power

The purpose of Tillich's writing on power in interwar Germany had been to encourage socialists to exercise it. In Tillich's judgment, the socialist tendency toward the renunciation of power grew out of their tendency to regard power and force as synonymous. The result was a dangerous utopianism that left the socialists unable to oppose more cynical groups like the Nazis. Tillich had tried to show that power was part of being and that its exercise in history was part of the self-actualization process with justice as the appropriate balancing of power.[19] Renunciation of power, on the other hand, was seen as an expression of the relationship of politics to eternity.

During the war Tillich's speaking on power and justice was immediately political. He sought solutions to the dangers of a power vacuum in Europe after the fall of Germany.[20] Power expressed the divine quality, and he thought that theologians as well as politicians should be concerned about its use and misuse. Justice and power implied each other and as a European political federation seemed more and more impossible, he hoped for at least an economic union that would provide social security as an antidote to the threat of Stalinism.

In 1952, a series of lectures in Nottingham, England, gave Tillich the opportunity to develop the concepts of love, power, and justice more fully than he had before. These lectures were given again at Princeton and at Union Theological Seminary in Virginia and eventually became the book *Love, Power, and Justice.* Continuity with his earlier work on power is obvious, but the immediate political context is absent. He develops the ontological analysis of power more fully and reaches back to the basic vision of reality he had found in Friedrich Schelling in his doctoral dissertation. In *Love, Power, and Justice* he wants to show that social ethics has to abandon the tendency to distrust power. Love and power have to be understood together if sensitive people are not to abandon politics to the cynics. The antimetaphysical bias of much American thought creates a tendency, following Ritschl, to divorce God's love from his power. For Tillich the reuniting task of love, power, and justice necessitates ontology as the descriptive analysis of being. Power was an ongoing concern of Tillich's, and his statements on the subject are, in part, his attempt to refute both cynics and perfectionists.

Tillich affirms the use of metaphorical language,[21] and he discusses power as the capacity of being to overcome nonbeing. Being, or the infinite, is present in everything finite and is the capacity of the finite to exist. Life is the expression of being in tension, risk, and decision. The power struggle is integral to life as every being seeks to expand. There is no escape from the power struggle except surrender of self-affirmation. In terms of political application, this means that the power struggle will continue, and no form of political organization can expect to overcome the dynamic competition or struggle of life. Power relationships exist and evolve continually within the human self, in nature, between people, and between groups. Life is shifting and dynamic, and the control of it invites resistance and rebellion. Despite the references to Sartre, Heidegger, and Nietzsche, it is the relatively unmentioned dynamism of Schelling's doctrine of the unity of the infinite and the finite that provides the framework of discussion, which Tillich summarizes as follows:

> Here we are at the roots of the concept of power. Power is the possibility of self-affirmation in spite of internal and external negation. It is the possibility of overcoming non-being.[22]

Translated into terms useful for political philosophy, power is at its roots the capacity to affirm one's purposes.

Tillich did not emphasize the independent power of ideas. Power is expressed not a priori but in reality: An idea has power if it shapes or interprets forces in history. By the mid-fifties, his religious social-ism was an idea with very little social expression. Consequently, his own theory of power led him not to advocate religious socialism. Its possibilities of realization had been negated, and forces in America were too strongly opposed to it. Religious socialism remained a vision, but his very realism dictated that this was a time for waiting. The revitalization of bourgeois life in America after the war led him to suppress his own vision and to work against specific expression of the demonic in society rather than expecting or advocating a new order. Still, it is a weakness of *Love, Power, and Justice* that the one paragraph on economics is so abstract that it obscures Tillich's con-cern for reducing inequality.[23]

Tillich accepted that in history there can be only fragmentary fulfillment. History itself continues to exhibit estrangement. God participates in that estrangement through agape and forgiveness, but not by compelling salvation. In creation, the creatures are free to be estranged. The unity of love and power is realized in eternity, and in history, only fragmentarily.

Practical Politics

Tillich's participation in postwar American politics, while less than his earlier activism, touched on most of the significant issues of the time. He dealt with the issues of nuclear weapons, civil rights, and repression from the right wing, and indirectly, his theology helped to open a new chapter in the rights of American conscien-tious objectors to war.

He served on Commission on the Christian Conscience and Weapons of Mass Destruction. The commission, organized by the Federal Council of Churches, stresses that the overriding issue be-fore it was how to avoid global war without surrendering to tyranny. The satanic temptation of preventive war must be put beyond the limits of tolerable policy, the commission concluded. Though it viewed war as tragic, the commission was not sanguine about agree-ments in 1950 to limit weapons development. Its primary agenda was to work on the moral and political level to overcome the issues of the cold war.

In its report, the commission reluctantly sanctioned the position of deterrence, but it warned against any first use of nuclear weapons or any attack that would drive the superpowers to use nuclear weapons. The commission, including Tillich, argued that if atomic weapons were used against the United States and its allies:

> We believe that it could be justifiable for our government to use them with all possible restraint to prevent the triumph of an aggressor.[24]

The report noted that even if some individuals would "rather be destroyed than to destroy in such measure," these pacifists ought not to urge such policies upon the government, which was responsible for the security and defense of all the people.[25]

In his own writing Tillich argued that a war fought with nuclear weapons could not be justified, and it was not permissible to enter a war with the intention of using nuclear weapons. Such a war, he said, would only bring mutual destruction and no avowed goal of the war could be fulfilled. He noted that the Western allies could, if they had the will, develop conventional armaments adequate to deter any communist invasion in Europe. Though he leaned toward a position of no first use of nuclear weapons as the commission had declared, he allowed the West some ambiguity in announcing such a policy. Until adequate conventional forces were created, he theorized, "maybe it was safer to keep the Communists uncertain about first use."[26] However, the logic of deterrence unequivocally meant:

> Our intention to answer any nuclear attack with nuclear weapons must be absolutely clear, and it must also be clear that we have the power to do so.[27]

The correspondence in the Harvard Archives indicates that Tillich was repeatedly requested by the American Friends Service Committee, the National Committee for a Sane Nuclear Policy, and other organizations to endorse their positions against weapons testing and for nuclear disarmament. He refused to give any of the organizations wholehearted support, and he especially resisted their pacifist leanings. However, he did sign a statement of the Committee for a Sane Nuclear Policy calling for arms control and the abolition of nuclear testing. The statement was published in the *New York Times* on

November 15, 1957, and included, in addition to Eleanor Roosevelt's, signatures of long-standing pacifists, antiwar activists, and religious leaders, one of whom was John Bennett, whose guidance Tillich sought on these questions. Reinhold Niebuhr, who was a little more of a cold warrior than Bennett, refrained from signing, though on most issues Bennett, Niebuhr, and Tillich agreed.

In 1955 Tillich had retired from Union and gone to Harvard. His Harvard secretary, Grace Leonard, was a member of SANE, and through her influence Tillich agreed to SANE's use in 1961 of a statement he had written several years before on the dangers of the hydrogen bomb. The statement summarizes well his general philosophical position on the threat of nuclear weapons:

> The increasing and apparently unlimited power of the means of self-destruction in the hands of men puts before us the question of the ultimate meaning of this development.
>
> The first point which comes to my mind is the possibility that it is the destiny of historical man to be annihilated not by a cosmic event but by the tensions in his own being and in his own history.
>
> The reaction to this possibility—this is the second point— should be the certainty that the meaning of human history, as well as of everyone's life within it, is not dependent on the time or the way in which history comes to an end. For the meaning of history lies above history.
>
> The third point is that everyone who is aware of the possibility of mankind's self-destruction must resist this possibility to the utmost. For life and history have an eternal dimension and are worthy to be defended against man's suicidal instincts which are socially as real as individually.
>
> The fourth point is that the resistance against the suicidal instincts of the human race must be done on all levels, on the political level through negotiations between those who in a tragic involvement force each other into the production of ever stronger means of self-destruction; on the moral level through a reduction of propaganda and an increase in obedience to the truth about oneself and the potential enemy; on the religious level through a sacred serenity and superiority over the preliminary concerns of life, and a new experience and a new expression of

the ultimate concern which transcends as well as determines man's historical existence.

The fifth point is that the resistance against the self-destructive consequences of man's technical control of nature must be done in acts which unite the religious, moral, and political concern, and which are performed in imaginative wisdom and courage.[28]

Tillich's philosophy of life prevented him from endorsing absolutely egalitarian measures, but it also protested against any measures that denied the full development of the capacity of people. He joined a committee for the defense of Professor Leo Koch who had been dismissed from the University of Illinois for his expression of views on sexual morality in 1960. He threw efforts behind a group working to repeal the McCarran Act. He signed statements calling for the abolition of the House Un-American Activities Committee. He lent the use of his name to groups promoting civil rights for blacks, such as the Committee to Salvage Talent sponsored by the National Scholarships Service and Fund for Negro Students. He joined Donald M. Fraser's committee working for open housing in 1965, and he joined the National Committee for Immigration Reform shortly before his death.[29]

The victory of John F. Kennedy in the election of 1960 rekindled Tillich's enthusiasm for politics. He was very moved when he was invited to join special guests at the inaugural festivities. In a letter to the young President, he admitted that the example of Kennedy in encouraging the arts and sciences had aroused in him a new interest in political thought. Later Tillich joined other religious leaders in urging caution during the Cuban missile crisis. His caution about the use of nuclear weapons brought him criticism from realists in both the United States and West Germany. He also signed a petition in support of the delivery of food to Communist China on April 18, 1962. The news of President Kennedy's assassination in 1963 reached him in Europe, and he reacted with the despair that characterized so many Americans who were counting on the directions in which Kennedy had begun to exhort the country.

Tillich supported the Johnson candidacy in 1964 and published a piece against Goldwater in *The Washington Post* just before the election. He attacked Goldwater's right-wing domestic policies and his militant saber rattling in foreign policy. He took his stand as a theologian:

> One should hesitate to reject a political candidate in the name of religion. For the political concern is preliminary and temporal, while religion is concerned with the ultimate and eternal meaning of life. Since, however, the eternal expresses itself in the temporal, e.g., in political ideas, and since such expression can be a distortion, religion sometimes must take a political side. Utterances of the Republican candidate and even more of forces supporting him show traits of such distortion: a disregard for economic and racial justice, an easy use of the warthreat, a production of false accusations and the suppression of free speech through them, the nourishing of hate towards foreign nations and the abuse of religion for all this. Therefore I feel, as a theologian, justified in calling for the defeat of the Republican ticket for the presidency.[30]

In 1965 the United States Supreme Court quoted from Tillich's *Systematic Theology* in a case about conscientious objection to war. The court ruled in favor of Daniel Andrew Seeger who claimed that he was entitled to the status of conscientious objector on the basis of his philosophical-religious position even though he was not a conventional theist. Before the Seeger case, the U.S. courts had restricted conscientious óbjector status to those who affirmed belief in a Supreme Being. Writing in volume 2 of *Systematic Theology*, Tillich argued that the affirmation of meaning is an affirmation of the "God above God" or the power of being even for those who cannot call upon the name of God.[31] This idea in Tillich's theology thus became one of the sources for a broader interpretation of religion by the Supreme Court and opened the way for many Americans to justify legally their pacifism. Tillich's thought implies rights of conscientious objection to particular wars, a stance to be rejected by the courts in the turmoil of the later sixties. Tillich even agreed to testify on behalf of the American Civil Liberties Union in a case involving the issue of broad religious, but not conventionally theistic, pacifism. There is irony in the nonpacifist Christian theologian's writing being used to win for non-Christian pacifists the right of conscientious objection to war. For Tillich, of course, such irony is central to human history.

As Tillich's social thought evolved in the two decades from 1945 to 1965, it changed with the thinking of his friends as had always been his pattern. Most important during this period was the influence of Reinhold Niebuhr and John Bennett. A note requesting political advice from Bennett in 1959 acknowledges his reliance upon his friend: "What shall I do? You are my father confessor in politics and religion!"[32]

Tillich had found a home in the Fellowship of Christian Socialists, and as it became less socialist in the postwar world, so did his thought. He summarized the evolution of the group, which eventually changed its name to Christian Action, in an address in 1955 as he was retiring from Union and moving to Harvard.[33] His reflections were personal, even to the point of commenting on Bennett's sister always remembering to bring him a bottle of beer at their semiannual retreats. Tillich commented that as the group had changed, he had been more conservative in his changes, meaning that he had retained more of his socialism and more enthusiasm for Marx than had other members. He noted that Niebuhr had changed the most, with Eduard Heimann close behind, while Winnifred Wygal remained closer to himself. Bennett, he placed as representing a balance between the extremes.[34]

This sketch of the changing positions of the members of the group indicated they no longer had a total worldview that included a necessary historical movement (socialism), a saving class (the proletariat), and the need for radical transformation (revolution). The group retained the struggle for a fragmentary realization of the Kingdom of God, but trusted that the final fulfillment was above and beyond history. In his address Tillich also affirmed that the healing of individuals and societies was interdependent and required both psychological and sociological analysis.[35]

The basic struggle against the demonic powers continued. The Leviathan of the spirit of industrial society still threatened the individual. The threat was seen not only in the subjection of some groups to misery, but also in the danger to those groups that dominated society, in terms of meaninglessness, accommodation, and subjection. Tillich found the tradition of religious socialism continuing in the politics of the group and in its search to articulate symbols that would encourage others to join in the struggle. He admitted some resignation, but recognized the need to work to keep the prophetic spirit alive in the church and society. His conclusion was an exhortation to: "Do it better!"[36]

XII.
Fulfillment

Tillich's great life work was his *Systematic Theology*. He had made notes for it before World War I. In 1925 in Marburg he actively planned its creation and even announced its publication for 1927. It was destined to be a post–World War II activity, however, and the volumes appeared in 1951, 1957, and 1963. During the fifties, completing the system was his central passion, and assistants helped him edit his classroom lectures to produce it. Students in New York, Boston, and Chicago listened to him working out the system in lectures and discussions. Parts III and IV were the Gifford lectures in Aberdeen, Scotland, of 1953 and 1954. Characteristically, any new or challenging idea would cause him to declare "I must revise my system." Several professors tell of Tillich walking with them in Boston, New York, or Chicago muttering that he was revising the whole system. Fundamentally, however, the structure of his thought remained unchanged. *Systematic Theology* incorporated his other writings and reaffirmed the persuasiveness of his earliest work on Schelling's philosophy prior to World War I.

Tillich's intention for his system is seen most clearly in his lectures on the history of Christian thought. He often portrayed Hegel and Schleiermacher, the two most influential theologians of the nineteenth century, as having produced great syntheses. They demonstrated that the truth of the Christian message was compatible with the modern mind.[1] Their syntheses were rejected by the middle of the nineteenth century, and the influence of Ritschlian synthesis, which replaced them, had faded by the end of the nineteenth century. The task at hand was, once again, to reconcile the modern mind and Christian truth. Unlike Karl Barth, Tillich did not want to emphasize the polemic against the synthesis of the modern mind and the gospel; he wanted to bring them together in a new way. He wanted to show that the Christian message is the answer to the modern tradition of self-critical humanism or existentialism.[2]

The human capacity for systematic thinking drove Tillich to express himself in a system. He noted various possibilities for theological writing from fragments to essays to systems and, finally, to *summae.* His own system was less complete than a *summae,* but it was complete enough to show the consequences of his method and complete enough to establish a correlation between his existential analysis of the contemporary situation and his ontological-mystical, theological answers to the questions of the situation.

Tillich wrote in continuity with one Christian tradition of philosophical theology. Many of his critics simply stand in different traditions and criticize him for using the tradition he does. A more profound criticism would be to show that he misused his own tradition or that the tradition was flawed in its essential components. This tradition of philosophical theology, articulated by Schelling and developed by Tillich, dominates the whole work from beginning to end.

From Schelling and the mystical-ontological tradition reaching back to Luther, Böhme, Augustine, Origen, John, and Paul, Tillich derived his drive to express the unity of the cosmos despite its diversity. The infinite is expressed in the finite, or being itself supports finite beings. Mysticism and ethics are reconciled, and theology must include both. Theology depends upon philosophy, and despite Tillich's efforts to distinguish them in his work, they collapse into each other. Existentialism depends upon previous insights of essentialism. As Tillich articulates his basic doctrine of God, the reconciliation of the structure of self and world, individualization and participation, dynamics and form, freedom and destiny, being and finitude, all depend upon the ontological tradition in which he stood.

Beneath the structure of his system stands a Christian—grasped by the question and reality of God—who will not let go of the modern situation. To reconcile his modern existentialist-essentialist mind with the Christian tradition, the five parts of the system correlate reason and revelation, being and God, existence and Christ, life and Spirit, history and the Kingdom of God. Despite particular problems, the beauty and power of the system are evident. The teachers of the church will, in the next decades, decide on its value for the life of the church; certainly at this point, for many, it stands as the most adequate expression of twentieth-century systematic theological work.

Analysis of the System's Social Thought

The "Introduction" to *Systematic Theology* sets forth the task of theologian as that of stating the truth of the Christian message and relating that truth to the contemporary situation. It is not the task of theologians to set forth a political program or a social philosophy. Tillich's work does not contain a section on government equivalent to John Calvin's Book IV, Chapter 20, in the *Institutes of the Christian Religion. Systematic Theology* is not political theology such as the current writing of the liberation theologians of the third world or the theologians of hope of present-day Germany. However, the second part of his task as a theologian requires analysis of the contemporary situation, including analysis of humanity's interpretation through sociology, political science, aesthetics, economics, psychology, literature, etc. He expresses it: "Thus theology is not concerned with the political split between East and West, but it *is* concerned with the political interpretation of this split."[3] He does not include a special section on Christian social ethics; rather, the system as a whole implies the ethic and reenforces his other writings on ethics.[4] In his design ethics and the other parts of the theological curriculum—philosophical theology, apologetics, dogmatics, and practical theology—are all incorporated into the categories of the system rather than remaining independent. Consequently, to show the social thought in *Systematic Theology* it is necessary to examine each part of the work for its political presuppositions and consequences, while keeping in view his other political and ethical writings.

The most important consequence of the political interpretation of the contemporary human situation is determinative for the shape of the system. In the opening pages Tillich makes it clear that to surrender theology to the situation is to make the mistake of the German Christians whom he had so bitterly opposed.[5] On the other hand, to pretend that theology is not involved in the situation leads to the dual mistakes of the politics of Barth: first ignoring Nazism and then absolutizing its opposition. The human situation, like an adequate theology, is dialectical. It is an expression of the essence of humanity and the existence of humanity. Theology must represent its essential teaching, but in response to the critically interpreted human situation.

Tillich's theology is written in dialogue with contemporary thinkers. Most of those he had in mind were humanistically educated skeptics. He wrote for the church, but for the church in conversation with contemporary skepticism about religious matters. Most of those for whom he wrote were not socialists or even politicians. Originally, the *Systematic Theology* was taken from his lectures at Union Theological Seminary, Harvard Divinity School, and the University of Chicago Divinity School, and consequently, it was addressed to the skepticism of theological students reflecting the modern situation. So though the introduction contains references to Hitler, Nazism, the East-West split, the ambiguities of history, religious nationalism, and political idolatry, it was written to suggest the outlines of the work, which attempts to express "the self-manifestation of the divine mystery."[6] The issue is not determining the appropriate form of social thought, but discovering how it is possible to overcome the split between modern consciousness and religious faith. Of course, for Paul Tillich, as for Alexander Solzhenitsyn,[7] the restoration of a meaningful faith to the Western world is of utmost political consequence. As Tillich's religious socialism was seeking the conditions for theonomy, so is his *Systematic Theology*.

An example of the correlation of his political philosophy with the structure of *Systematic Theology* is the deriving of the criteria for theology from the Great Commandment: "The Lord, our God, the Lord is one; and you shall love the Lord your God with all your heart, and with all your soul and with all your mind, and with all your strength."[8] God, as ultimate concern, is the abstract translation of this commandment, and both of Tillich's two formal criteria of theology derive from it. The Protestant principle, which was central to religious socialism's protest against all forms of political idolatries, also derives from this commandment. Tillich's politics and his theology are of one foundation.

Part I of Tillich's system is his epistemology. It is in some ways the most difficult part of the system for the nonspecialist in theology to understand. Since for Tillich epistemology, the science of knowing, is part of ontology, the science of being, it is appropriate for most readers to study Part II, "Being and God," before undertaking Part I. There is one significant aspect of Part I for Tillich's social philosophy. He teaches that: "Cognitive dehumanization has produced actual dehumanization."[9]

He argues that the victory of technical reason over ontological reason has resulted in humanity's being subjected to technical manipulation. In this argument he follows his friend from the Institute for Social Research Max Horkheimer who had traced the victory of technical reason over ontological reason in *The Eclipse of Reason*. [10] The victory, Tillich points out, encouraged the treatment of human beings as means rather than ends. It undercut any adequate defense of human values and prepared the ground for the erosion of human values in the societies dominated by both liberal capitalist consumerism and Stalinist terror. The movements of romanticism, vitalism, and existentialism all protested against controlling technical knowledge in the realm of epistemology and the controlling technical manipulation of people in society. As those movements avoided grounding in the self-manifestation of being, however, they were left without criteria of truth and without connections to the values that they wanted to defend. Tillich describes the world of liberal capitalism as the world of empty autonomy, and he labels the world of Marxist dominance a world of destructive heteronomy:

> The double fight against an empty autonomy and a destructive heteronomy makes the quest for a new theonomy as urgent today as it was at the end of the ancient world. The catastrophe of autonomous reason is complete.[11]

Tillich does not despise technical reason; his point is that it must be guided by the tradition of ontological reason, which runs from Parmenides through Hegel, for the fulfillment of human purposes. Ontological reason explicates the rational character of reality and shows the ends for which technical reason ought to be used. Ontological reason is reason in the service of God for explicating the Logos. Under the conditions of human existence, reason is subject to the polarities of the conflicts between autonomy and heteronomy, relativism and absolutism, and formalism and emotionalism. The reunion of these poles is found in revelation, where the power of being itself is encountered. "Revelation is the manifestation of the depth of reason and the ground of being."[12]

For Tillich there is no conflict between revelation, as the disclosing of the depths of being, and reason, as the explication of the structures of being. Reason drives to the answers of revelation and depends upon revelation for its completeness. Social healing, the restoration of theonomy or the living in God's saving power, demands that reason and revelation be understood as interrelated. Revelation cannot be heteronomy; rather, it fulfills the reason of the autonomous thinker in ecstatic, transforming reason.

Even in this formal writing on epistemology Tillich returns to the problem of uniting theory and practice.[13] He concedes that under conditions of existence the two cannot be perfectly joined, though both the Fourth Gospel and Karl Marx point to the necessity of doing the truth to learn the truth. Humanity practices the way it sees the world, and Tillich's chapter on epistemology is an argument for seeing the world as dependent upon God. Theory and practice seem to be imperfectly joined in history just as salvation and revelation are only imperfectly realized in the lives of those who are possessed of them.

The chapter criticizes many schools of theology and philosophy and defines many of Tillich's terms quite carefully. It presents, in summary, the argument that Christian theology grounded in revelation can be understood reasonably. Both the theology and the reason are distinctively those of Tillich, the existentialist student of Schelling representing the Augustinian-Lutheran mystical side of the classical Christian tradition. Fittingly, the necessity of existentialist commitment and mystical intuition by the theologian is also part of the argument of the chapter. The circle is complete.

Part II of the system is relatively empty of social analysis. The catastrophes of the twentieth century are in the background preventing the credibility of theories of rational providence. The providence of God is an "in spite of." Even though the theologian or philosopher cannot escape the relativity of his historical situation, the fact that "he is grasped by the idea of God is not dated."[14] The reflections on ontology in the section on being and on being itself in the section on the reality of God áre not heavily influenced by social philosophy. There is a discussion of love, power, and justice, which summarizes the book *Love, Power, and Justice* but adds nothing new.[15]

The discussion of the reality of God indicates that the exposition of the social consequences of the theology will appear under the categories of existence in Part V. There is a vision in the discussion in Part II of the unity of the world in God that prohibits the emergence of a crusade mentality on religious grounds. It also contains a rejection of individual escapism of social consequences of the contemporary situation. Tillich's explicit statement of the dependence of the individual upon society is clear: "The destiny of the individual cannot be separated from the destiny of the whole in which it participates."[16] The emergence of exclusive monotheism is associated with the consciousness of the principles of justice. So, though this part of the system is not social theology, the dependence of ethics on ontology, for which he argued in his doctoral dissertation, is still in view.

Tillich's first Gifford Lectures at Aberdeen in 1953 were published in 1957 as volume 2 of *Systematic Theology* containing Part III of his system, "Existence and Christ." In an introduction he refined his use of being as the fundamental concept for systematic theology and defended his method of apologetic theology. The writing is more polemical than in the first volume. It is as if the criticism of the first volume had freed him from any illusions that his theology would be generally acceptable to the whole church. In the second volume he is clearer about his personal theological convictions. The analysis of existence is clearly that of a theologian whose Christology is dialectically related to the analysis of existence. He is, in this volume, neither a philosopher in a detached sense nor simply a spokesman for the Christian answer to the problems of existence. His own creative, individual stamp is upon the writing in both the presentation of the questions of existence and in the answers derived from the christological tradition.

Except for a few references, the volume is apolitical.[17] Neither the issue of Jesus' relationship to political issues and parties nor the political dimension of human existence is explored in depth.

In analyzing the estrangement of human existence, Tillich spends some paragraphs on the problem of collective guilt. "There is no collective guilt," he argues, for the group does not decide; individuals within the group make the decisions.[18] The individual participates in the destiny of the group but is guilty only of the crimes committed as an individual and, only in an indirect sense, of the contribution made to the destiny of the group. Tillich allows for a weak sense of the responsibility of each individual, even one who resisted the group, for the actions of the group. In a similar way, members of opposing groups may have contributed also, to the destiny of a group in which crimes were committed. His own experience as a post–World War I German is evident here. By denying "collective guilt," he wants to restrain victorious nations from exploiting their victories by punishing whole nations. He points to the difference between a group and a person and argues that the group has no decision-making center from which the guilt of all in the group could be assumed. His denial of "collective guilt" is weakened somewhat because of his necessity to affirm the contributions of individuals to the groups or nations to which they belong. His recommendations during World War II are consistent with this analysis. He had argued that all of those connected with Nazism should be deplaced from power and punished, but all Germans should not be punished because of an assertion of "collective guilt."

Parts IV and V of Tillich's system appeared as volume 3 in 1963, six years after Part III. The criticism of his Christology in volume 2 resulted in the introduction to volume 3 being the most tentative of any of the introductions. The system was complete, but he noted its fragmentary character and admitted that much of the work was inadequate. In these later years, he had become worried about his health and anxious about whether or not he would ever complete the system. Though other work would follow, his vocation was fulfilled with the publication of this final volume of *Systematic Theology*. In less than two years he would die. The final volume was dedicated, "For Hannah, The Companion of My Life." In their closing years their relationship had mellowed somewhat and a reconciliation had taken place. The reconciliation participated, however, in the ambiguity of life that was the theme of volume 3. After his death, Hannah's resentment would boil over in the publication of her fragmentary biography, *From Time to Time,* revealing her anger at their alienation.

Part IV, "Life and the Spirit," presented his existential philosophy of life and his answer to the ambiguous nature of life in the analysis of the reality of Spiritual Presence. It is the longest part of the system, and it reveals the mystical roots of Tillich's thought more clearly than any other part. The Spiritual Presence "is the aspect of God ecstatically present in the human spirit and implicitly in everything which constitutes the dimension of the spirit."[19] The length and power of his writing on the spirit, along with his critique of christocentric theologies, certainly permits the observation that the third person of the Trinity seems to dominate the second. The lengthy discussion of the church is carried out under the terms of the analysis of the Spiritual Presence in all humanity and in specific Christian congregations.

Tillich explores psychoanalysis, existentialism, the church, culture, morality, and religion under the rubrics of the ambiguity of life and the Spiritual Presence. Often the discussion in the volume is a repetition from his smaller, less technical works *Biblical Faith and Ultimate Reality, The Dynamics of Faith,* and *Love, Power, and Justice.* Aside from the discussion of social ethics and the repetition of discussions about love and justice, there are only a dozen or so references to issues of social philosophy. The terms demonic and theocracy reveal their origins in the religious socialist movement, but there is no argument for a particular social realization. The discussion of theory and praxis obscures its importance in the circles of Marxist-inspired social criticism. The issues of social philosophy, Tillich decided, should be examined under the categories of historical existence, so they were put into Part V of the system. Tillich's criticism of Protestantism's overemphasis of male symbolism and his own hints for the correction of this distortion, though brief, may be some of the most helpful insights from the volume for the theological work of the 1980s.[20]

Tillich's system comes to its end and its fulfillment in the discussion of the ambiguity of history and the Kingdom of God in Part V. Tillich regards the Kingdom of God as "a most important" symbol; he does not call it *the* most important. Especially it is a critical symbol for ecclesiastical and political life. The pressures of ecclesiastical life toward absolutism have eclipsed the symbol, which is a guard against that very absolutism. Also, the Kingdom of God is a difficult symbol because it has both historical and transhistorical aspects. Despite the difficulties, Tillich affirms its revival in the social-gospel movement in America and identifies its importance in his own articulation of religious socialism in Germany.[21] He looks for its reinstatement as a powerful symbol in the dialogue with Eastern religions.[22] Also, the memory that Jesus' message was the preaching of the Kingdom of God and that every repetition of the Lord's Prayer petitions for its coming should encourage its revival despite its difficulty. The emerging of political theologies and liberation theologies since Tillich's writing confirms his hopes for the revival of this symbol even if these theologies have not always guarded the concept from utopianism.

Tillich's writing on history passionately rejects philosophies of history characterized as progressive, utopian, transcendental, and nonhistorical. In his view humanity is in history, and no one escapes its influence. The political element is central in history, and the fight for freedom is carried out most significantly in the political realm. Marxist interpretations of history are not obvious, and even the importance of economics is downplayed. History is life in existence and reflects all of the ambiguities of life. There are structures, but human freedom and chance can undo or overthrow structures. There is a drive in history toward centralization, newness, fulfillment, and universality, says Tillich, but these characteristics of the Kingdom of God are only partially realized in history. The Kingdom of God is the answer to the agonies of history.

Humanity's political organization reveals the drive toward centralization and universality in the building of empires. The empires express a particular vocational consciousness, such as Great Britain's attempt to represent Christian humanism, as well as the will to power. But the vocational consciousness of imperial groups is resisted by various consciousnesses of the oppressed. Even in the ruling group, the necessities of ruling come into conflict with the vocational consciousness. These ambiguities prevent any imperial power from surviving. They have their day and pass.

Historical self-creativity is expressed as new forces and new ideas emerge to oppose the old. If a system is not structured to allow the new to emerge, pressures and contradictions build to the point of revolution. "There are situations in which only a revolution (not always a bloody one) can achieve the breakthrough to a new creation.[23] Tillich notes the dangers of revolutionary purpose being betrayed by the dynamics of the revolutionary process. He is no romanticizer of revolution, but he explicitly rejects the ecclesiastical tendency to oppose revolution. Paul's caution about opposing government in Romans 13, he argues, was directed against apocalyptic enthusiasts, not against revolutionary forces about to install a new order to replace a decaying one. Revolution, like empire, participates in historical ambiguity.

As did his colleague Reinhold Niebuhr, Tillich aims for liberation from both cynicism and utopianism in his writing on politics in the *Systematic Theology*.[24] He advocates the politics of responsibility, in Max Weber's sense of responsibility. History produces drives to transcend its ambiguities, and these drives are expressed in mythologies of the "third stage" or "Third Reich" or "Age of Reason" or "Classless Society." In history, however, these myths fail. Even limited attempts at absolutism must fail as, for example, a political party in Russia or the church in Rome. Though the failures can produce cynicism, Tillich urges action against the various forces of the demonic.

Democracy is also an ambiguous political expression, but it is the best way of protecting human freedom within an organized group.[25] In modern society, Tillich argues, freedom must be preserved in the political sphere or it will be lost in other realms as well. Techniques of representation, control of communication, and party bureaucracies reduce the freedom of the individual to participate creatively in society. Majority rule can be misused to deprive minorities of expression. Democracy in practice is fully ambiguous, Tillich acknowledges, but when contrasted with various forms of totalitarianism, democracy is clearly more successful than dictatorships in nurturing individual creativity. Democracy's tendency toward mass conformity, nonetheless, presents a very real danger to creativity, in some cases even more danger than does an absolutism that elicits opposition.[26]

The risk of this emphasis on the ambiguity of history and fragmentary fulfillment in history is that it will lead to a politics of complacency. The tension between the presence of the Kingdom of God in the achievements of authentic democracy and the not-yet-fulfilled Kingdom of God in the failures of democracy is difficult to maintain even when the theoretical need for such tension is perceived. Satisfied forces in the church and in government will pervert the tension into satisfaction with the status quo. Tillich emphasizes this danger in the *Systematic Theology,* making one of his infrequent references to the Marxist philosopher Ernst Bloch and his "restatement of the 'principle of hope.' " The emergence of hope in opposition to smug complacency Tillich regards as a victory for "the fighting Kingdom of God." In discussing Bloch, he refers to "movements of expectation," which was his own central term for socialism in *The Socialist Decision.* [27] He cannot leave the discussion, however, without again pointing to the tendency in such movements to forget the presence—even if fragmentary—of the reality of the Kingdom of God. Elsewhere during the same period as the writing of the *Systematic Theology,* Tillich called for the victory of the "spirit of utopia" over utopianism.[28] Here in Part V of the system we have essentially the same point: The Kingdom of God as the Spiritual Presence of God is real in human history; it drives humanity to fulfill creativity, universality, and community, but the fulfillment does not come in history. The ambiguities of history, including the fragmentary realization of the Kingdom, drive humanity toward answers that are found in the Kingdom as the end of history or as eternal life. A consideration of the beauty and persuasiveness of Tillich's discussion of eternal life is beyond the purpose of this study.

The *Systematic Theology* achieves its aim, which was to present a synthesis of Christian essentialism in terms of its mystical-ontological roots with existentialism as it emerged particularly in the later Schelling. The apologetic power of the system is impressive, especially to those inclined toward the mystical side of Protestant theology but who desire a realistic ethic. The system cannot be faulted for doing what it expressly intended. There are, of course, other theological traditions, and it is proper for theologians in those traditions to write their own apologetics. They may produce systems that have a higher Christology or that rely more on biblical terminology, but it is doubtful that they could articulate a more powerful presentation of God as "being itself" or as "Spiritual Presence" than Tillich has. His discussion of the ambiguity of history and the Kingdom of God has lasting value, and he has contributed to the restoration of the symbol of the Kingdom of God as the central symbol for Christian thinking about society.

The *Systematic Theology* was written in conversation with Tillich's sources, but mainly for American students of theology in the 1950s and 1960s. These were the students who lived during the Eisenhower era, but at Union Theological Seminary, Harvard Divinity School, and the Divinity School of the University of Chicago, these students were politically following Governor Adlai Stevenson, Senator Hubert Humphrey, and, in 1960, Senator John F. Kennedy. Their political philosophers helped shape the Americans for Democratic Action and participated in the cold war as liberal democrats. The students were neither revolutionaries nor socialists. Tillich's ideology or political worldview at this time did not support the cold war as did the perspective of his friend Reinhold Niebuhr, but he and Niebuhr were allies in the struggle against forces in the United States that threatened creativity and freedom, such as their campaign to abolish the House Un-American Activities Committee. Tillich supported nonideological solutions to practical political problems. His thought does not reflect any acceptance of laissez-faire capitalism, for example, but can be regarded as supporting mixed economic solutions. He held to a personal vision of religious socialism and the contemporary meaning of theonomous society, but his listeners and readers were not interested and he muted the references to it in the *Systematic Theology*. During the Eisenhower years in the United States, the advocacy of religious socialism would have been utopian, and he was determined not to be a utopian. If the seminaries had contained more third-world students who were conscious revolutionaries, more blacks, or more radical feminists, his theology would have been written with them more in mind. As he wrote in the U.S. he did not have a proletariat in view. Without a proletariat, social theology becomes—as his did—a theology to fight against dehumanizing forces in the society rather than for the restructuring of society.

Dehumanization in the Technical Society

While welcoming technical development, Tillich feared the ˙˷humaniz·ng effects of modern technological society. In an essay r·lebracing the founding of Christian Action in a volume that served as a tribute to Reinhold Niebuhr, Tillich tried to show a way to resist the process of dehumanization.[29] He saw the existentialism movement in Kierkegaard, Marx, and Nietzsche as a protest against the reduction of a person to a thing. The protest was profound, but it failed. For different reasons, he said, Sartre's existentialism and psychoanalysis failed. Also, the conservative defense of modern society and the retreat into the contemporary church failed to preserve humanity.

Tillich hoped for the development of groups that could resist the mass conformity in modern society that compelled people to surrender their personal creativity. In the essay he recommended to groups like Christian Action, the successor to the Fellowship of Socialist Christians, a retreat from and an attack on modern society. The "partial nonparticipation" in the structure of modern society, he argued, was best grounded in the "new Reality" represented in the Christian message and elsewhere. The retreat was an affirmation of the religious reservation about the world; the attack could be expressed in a "rebellion of life" against forces that degraded the person. The attack also had to continue the fight for social justice. As Nietzsche represented the rebellion of life and Marx the struggle for social justice against capitalist society, so Kierkegaard represented the seeking of the ultimate roots of personal identity. Withdrawal from the clutches of technical society was necessary if one were to hope to act against that society. And while the withdrawal was to religious resources, the attack was one in which allies were sought within technical society to fight its dehumanizing aspects. The person could finally be defended only by a "personal encounter with the ground of everything personal."[30]

Tillich was, of course, himself part of technical society, and his transcendence was only partial. His refusal to accept the conditions of contemporary socioreligious life is clearly seen in the essay. In fact, this statement shows perhaps more clearly than the *Systematic Theology* the part of the modern mind with which he correlated his theology. His correlations were with the modern mind in rebellion against the dominating trends.

His acceptance of much of technical-scientific development is seen in his celebration of the new perspectives coming to humanity through space exploration. The space program harnessed to military competition strengthened antidemocratic tendencies within the United States. Yet, he affirmed the program because it expressed the creativity of humanity. It contained immense dangers, but the threat of danger was not a reason to stop development. Eventually, "space exploration will be judged in the light of the meaning of life in all its dimensions."[31] The political process would sort out the priorities of the nation as reflected by the operative forces in the system. He hoped that the humanistic elements in society would insist on values other than those simply residing in the drive to push as far as possible. The nonhumanistic forces in society were prevalent, but because they were not self-sufficient, rebellion against them could be expected. Tillich did not live long enough to see the beginnings of mass revolt by American young people against the technological system or to see their defeat and return to quietism. His judgment that the political system itself would arrange the priorities of the nation regarding space exploration was correct. Like all other exceptionally creative human endeavors, space exploration caused his spirit to soar, but the program itself remained ambiguous.

Anti-Semitism and Zionism

Tillich always spoke prophetically as well as ontologically on his return visits to Germany after the war. On the occasion of his reception of the Peace Prize from the German Publisher's Association in Frankfurt in 1962, he spoke of "Frontiers." He spoke of his own life of crossing various boundaries both intellectual and political. He urged West Germans to cross the border between East and West Germany intellectually and spiritually and to open themselves to the humanistic elements in the communist-occupied countries of East Europe. He also expressed the need to recognize limits and argued that frontiers established limits. He advocated acceptance of the frontier dividing East and West Germany. Attempts to dissolve this frontier politically, he said, would only heighten the dangers of a nuclear holocaust that could never be justified. The crossing of frontiers emotionally and intellectually could reduce anxiety concerning the reality on the other side and promote peace.[32] Germany must learn to recognize its limits and to accept its historical situation as established by the world division between East and West. The failure of Germany to have peace in the twentieth century, Tillich charged forthrightly, rested in the German failure to develop a sense of national purpose within finite limits. This development of a sense of purpose and recognition of the nation's finite limits were the prerequisites of peace.[33]

Also exceptionally bold were Tillich's lectures in 1953 on "The Jewish Question: Christian and German Problem" at the Deutschen Hochschule für Politik in Berlin. His audience received the lectures very soberly and, as he had hoped, searched themselves. He faced the problem of German guilt directly even though he knew most Germans did not want to think about guilt. His analysis here goes further than what he said about guilt later that same year in his lectures at Aberdeen. To his German audience he pointed out five types of guilt.[34] Primarily guilt meant that one was directly responsible for the evil act. A second type of guilt was the failure to act responsibly. In a third sense there was the guilt of suppressing knowledge. There was also the guilt of forgetting one's responsibility for the past. The fifth type of guilt he analyzed was more conscious than the unconscious mechanisms of three and four. It was the type of guilt that righteously asserted: We have done wrong, but we have been punished, and all is equal. In Tillich's judgment, only some Germans were guilty in the first sense of the deliberate act. Many more were guilty of sensing what was happening and failing to act. Indeed, he affirmed his own guilt in not acting more boldly before 1933 as the situation deteriorated. He considered the final three forms of guilt to be operative throughout broad sections of the German population, with very destructive psychological consequences.[35]

He used in his lectures the analysis of anti-Semitism and anti-Judaism that he had written during the war.[36] Even though the church's official positions were better described as anti-Judaism, Christianity must bear responsibility for nurturing anti-Semitism. In looking at the issue of the guilt of Jews for the death of Jesus he wrote:

> It is worth looking at this reproach in the light of our analysis of the concept of guilt. One, then, immediately sees the absurdity of this accusation. None of the concepts of guilt which I have mentioned can be applied to this phenomenon.[37]

Tillich's recommendations for the purging of anti-Semitism from the Christian churches involved the cleansing of all church publications, the emphasis of the Old Testament, the abandonment of the active mission to the Jews, the sharing of Jewish and Christian services, the joining together in the struggle for social justice, the acceptance of Jewry as representing a prophetic critique of Christianity, and the continuing of the theological dialogue with Jews about their expected Messiah and Christianity's symbol of the second coming of Christ.

The analysis he presented of Judaism as a German problem was new and went further than anything he had said earlier. First he developed at length ways in which Germans and Jews were similar. Both groups were heirs to a prophetic reformation, regarded living space as a metaphysical problem, and had a higher than usual sense of being chosen. Both groups were characterized by intense inner spiritual struggles containing self-rejection and anxious self-affirmation, were surprisingly adaptive to other cultures, and exhibited an estrangement of leaders from their mass populations. "The structural similarities between the German and the Jewish character to which I have pointed, lead to both strong attraction and extreme repulsion."[38]

Next Tillich surveyed economic and sociological explanations of anti-Semitism and argued that "systematic anti-Semitism is an invention of naturalistic anthropology of the late nineteenth century."[39] Expressed in biological theories of race, naturalistic anthropology played into the hands of totalitarianism, which had to create an enemy to further its own program. The arguments given to justify anti-Semitism were irrational and contradictory. "There is nothing more absurd, nothing more irrational than political anti-Semitism."[40] The mass psychoses that gripped Germany under Nazism reduced the anti-Semite to the role that he had assigned the Jew, that is, something less than truly human.[41]

In seeking an answer for Germany, Tillich returned to his typology of guilt and expressed what was tantamount to a collective analysis. Every German needed to acknowledge responsibility for what had happened and participate in repentance. The stereotyping of Jews had to be overthrown and replaced by sober judgments of the empirical realities.[42] Germans would have to overcome their sense of inferiority, which produced arrogance, again requiring sober judgments. Finally, Germany had to be reintegrated into Christian humanistic culture. The defeat of paganism in Germany would enable Germans to accept the prophetic contribution of Judaism.[43]

Tillich's lectures, published in German and in English by *Jewish Social Studies,* are among the deepest of his writings. By themselves, these lectures may give the impression that Tillich stereotyped both Germans and Jews, but his other writing dispells that mistaken idea. Long acquaintance with Jews and appreciation for Jewish philosophers conditioned him to become one of the best friends that Judaism had among the ranks of Christian theologians. In addressing his audience in Berlin, he said that the only witness Christians finally had to Jews that the "new being" had actually appeared was their own expression of it in their lives. He hoped that the power of the new being in Christianity would "destroy the demonism of anti-Semitism" and that a new relationship between Jews and Christians would emerge.[44]

For most of Tillich's life, Judaism was the faith of a dispersed people. He had known Jews as a people without their own space, a people primarily of time. After the establishment of Israel, he joined the American Christian Palestine Committee, which sought to promote understanding for Israel in the U.S. In comments on his acceptance of Zionism as a legitimate expression of Judaism, he noted how his own position had changed.[45] Assimilation had ended in disaster. The average Jew, who was not a suffering prophet, needed space for destiny and protection. Israel was a contemporary political reality and participated in the historical ambiguities of justice and injustice. Support for Israel did not mean "the fulfillment of the symbol of the Promised Land." Israel was a state, but the prophetic minority of Jews remained not only within Israel but also in the Diaspora. "Therefore, an identification of Israel as a nation with the nature and destiny of the people of time is wrong."[46] Tillich's support for Israel's security as a state did not depend on illusions regarding the internal affairs of Israel or upon apocalyptic arguments. Rather, he recognized the reality of the failure of Europe to protect Jews and the reality of their state in Palestine, and he urged their protection. His counsel to the Germans on the occasion of speaking to them of their guilt serves equally as well as counsel to the Jews in concluding this discussion of his thought about Israel: Accept finite borders and develop vocational consciousness and security. In a negotiating process, he said, borders could be found that would recognize the vitalities of the parties to the dispute and promote relative, though never absolute, security. His whole argument rules out a Zionism based upon biblical legalism regarding borders or absolute solutions.[47]

Peace on Earth

On February 18, 1965, Tillich delivered a short paper entitled "Peace on Earth." The event was a convocation of the Center for the Study of Democratic Institutions occasioned by Pope John

XXIII's 1963 encyclical *Pacem in Terris*. Cold warriors had previously been critical of Tillich's rejection of the use of nuclear weapons to defend Berlin, James Reston and Dean Rusk regarding his position as unrealistic.[48] However, here in this essay—one of his last on politics—his faithful realism was still evident.

He praised the Pope's action in issuing the statement and its emphasis on "the ultimate principle of justice."[49] However, most of his essay was a critique of the encyclical followed by his own state ment of hope for the struggle toward peace. He found the encyclical too limited in vision. This search for peace, he argued, must be more open to traditions other than Western Christian humanism. The encyclical obscured the injustice that would result from resistance to injustice. Power was not sufficiently dealt with in the encyclical, particularly the necessary ambiguities of power. The encyclical also obscured the degree to which moral expectations for groups were different from those of individuals. Finally, said Tillich, the appeal should not have been addressed moralistically to "all men of good will," but to all people, for evil and good are mixed in all humanity.

The encyclical was too close to utopianism for Tillich. Hope had to be grounded in realities. Tillich could see hope for peace in the fear of mutual destruction, the technical unity of humanity in space conquest, the increasing worldwide dialogue on many fronts, the development of some world legal structures, and a few signs of emerging consensus or communal *eros*.[50] He did not, however, hope for a final stage of peace on earth within history. He did hope for fragmentary victory over structures of evil, of which war was one of the greatest. Too easy speeches for peace created cynicism, he thought. The struggle for peace had to be continued even when the signs of probable failure were prevalent. He argued that, with a hope for victory, people could work for peace in particular situations even though they knew total peace would elude them. Rejecting utopianism and affirming hope he urged the conference to begin its work.

The critique of the encyclical is very representative of Tillich's political ethics. The positions of faithful realism, attack on utopianism, emphasis on power, distinction in morals between groups and individuals, the ambiguity of human existence are all continuous themes in his political writing. Sharing a Christian humanism with the Pope, Tillich nonetheless draws from his Lutheran heritage a realism that the encyclical lacks, and he looks for hope not so much in moral exhortation but in empirical political realities.

Buddhism and Democracy

Tillich's final lecture, given in Chicago on October 12, 1965, was "The Significance of the History of Religions for the Systematic Theologian." Later that evening he suffered a heart attack, and ten days later he died. His last lecture summarized reflections on the history of religion that he had gained from the joint seminar he and Mircea Eliade had led at Chicago and from the experience of his 1960 trip to Japan. It reflected also his first doctoral dissertation. His experience in Japan and his dialogue with Buddhism had already influenced his Bampton Lectures at Columbia in 1961.[51] His final lecture argued for the need of the systematic theologian to take seriously the data of the history of religions for theological work. Actually *Systematic Theology* had included considerable reflection on material from the history of religions, but he was calling here for a greater emphasis on the variety of religious experience. His own work had been in dialogue more with secular problems, and the dialogue needed to be in both directions. His sharp critique of the secular theologians and the death-of-God movement was informed by his late-life deeper engagement with non-Christian religions, especially Buddhism.[52] The lecture counterattacked the critics of religion whether they were radical-secular theologians or Barthian theologians. His own understanding of the interpretation of religion demanded that it be seen in its total cultural context and that its relationship to economic and political structures be explicated.[53]

On his trip to Japan in the summer of 1960, he had explored Shinto, Buddhism, Christianity, Confucianism, and the new religions in the cultural situation of Japan. His report on that trip is full of political analysis as well as theological reflections.[54] It was a tense time as violence had accompanied the arrival of presidential envoy James Hagerty, and President Eisenhower's expected visit had been cancelled.

He had lectured on "Religious Socialism" and "The Spiritual

Foundations of Democracy" as well as on many theological and philosophy of religion subjects.[55] His lectures on the foundations of democracy stressed that democracy was dependent upon "the development of the principle of individuality in the subconscious of at least the leading group, ideally the whole nation."[56] He could not find in Japan, permeated as it was with Buddhism, this sense of individuality that had grown out of the particular religious heritage of the West.[57] Democracy was a fragile corrective of the tendency toward the dehumanization of tyranny. It appeared only seldom in Christianity, and he could not find it in Buddhism or Islam.[58] Democracy was limited and threatened from all sides, but it was particularly threatened in Asia where it was a recent import and where the necessary spiritual foundation seemed to be lacking.

For Tillich, the creativity of humanity was the fulfillment of its destiny, and he saw democracy not as an absolute, but as the best way to protect that creativity. He recognized the threat to creativity of mass conformism in democracy, and he saw the tendency toward a secular conformism operating in Japan as it did in the United States. Despite the Japanese commitment to democracy, he considered it particularly threatened there.

This encounter with living Buddhism emphasizes again the continuity of the life and passion of Tillich. He was heir to Hegel and Schelling who reflected the burst of freedom contained in the French Revolution. Rejecting Hegel's understanding of world religions, he continued Hegel's passion for relating religion and politics. Tillich viewed politics as the practical expression of the religious depths of a people and the task in history as still that of Schelling: to find a way of human freedom.

Before he died Tillich had accepted a post as a philosopher of society at the New School for Social Research in New York. As Hannah Tillich put it: "The golden gates of Berlin, mirrored in New York, called again. He accepted."[59] He did not live to assume the post. His family selected as a final resting place for his remains a park bearing his name in New Harmony, Indiana. He was interred among the trees on the site of a German religious-socialist community, which had also been the site briefly of Robert Owen's socialist community. Tillich's spirit and vision belong to eternity; he could not have accepted all of the aspects of either the Harmonists or Owen's socialist communes, but certainly their attempts to create humane conditions were part of the fighting Kingdom of God as was his life.

Conclusion

As a whole Tillich's social thought includes very little from which I would dissent. His early 1918–1919 attempt to merge socialism and Christianity was a little too enthusiastic, but he realized this and, in his own writings, dealt with the problems and ambiguities of socialism. A revitalized socialism would have been the only force adequate to resist Nazism within Germany in the 1930s. He made the contribution to that attempted revitalization of which he was capable. His defeat in 1933 at the hands of the Nazis was the defeat not only of socialism, but temporarily of the civilized world. From 1933 to 1945 his continued opposition to Nazism and his pleading for a humane policy toward Germany represented social wisdom. In the twenties and thirties religious socialism was an appropriate re-sponse in terms of Christian social ethics. It met the three criteria of ethical reflection for Tillich: It was an approximation in theory of love and justice, it corresponded to social theory and moral princi-ple, and it was a decision fitting to the time and situation. American political realities and the outbreak of the cold war presented him with a situation in which the advocacy of religious socialism did not fit. He retained it as an expression of the meaning of love and justice and as his own developed social theory, but he accepted that it did not suit postwar America. Though he would write in 1952: "If the prophetic message is true, there is nothing 'beyond religious social-ism.' "[60]

After the war, Tillich turned to his basic theoretical work. *System-atic Theology* was his attempt to overcome the split between the modern mind and the Christian mind that was so fatal to human freedom and creativity. He muted his own political statements to reserve his energies for this most important work. Confronting a time in which the resistance of evil was more appropriate than expec-tation of a new future, he continued to participate in major issues more than the typical professor, but much less actively than the socialist theoretician of earlier years. For example, he granted permission to use his name as a sponsor for a rally against the Vietnam War when he himself could not be present.[61]

If he had been more aware of the suffering in the third world, his *Systematic Theology* would have contained more of the passion of *The Socialist Decision*. He did not address directly the questions of these forgotten poor. In fact, in his world travels, he did not see them except possibly in Egypt and Mexico. He remained a theologian of the Northern Hemisphere wrestling with the questions of skepticism. However, writings from Germany when he had a proletariat in view may prove to be very useful to third-world theologians who want to structure their own theologies of liberation. In those writings he stripped away the pretensions of bourgeois society so thoroughly that they can never be recovered. *The Religious Situation, The Socialist Decision,* and *Love, Power, and Justice,* together with the third volume of *Systematic Theology,* are more accessible to the critics of capitalism than to its defenders. North Americans who want to enter into a dialogue with third-world critics probably could do this more sympathetically from Tillich's theological perspective than from any of the major alternatives.

Tillich's work unites the best elements of Christian realism and liberation theologies. He did not fall prey to the tendency in Christian realism to support ideological anticommunism. Neither did he make the mistake of thinking that the longed-for fulfillment of social justice would be unambiguously realized. Christian realists may prefer the third volume of *Systematic Theology* and liberation theologians *The Socialist Decision,* but to understand Tillich these works must be read together and in full recognition of the difference between Germany in 1933 and America in 1963. Tillich's name for his position was "Faithful Realism." In the 1920s and 1930s it was a philosophy of expectation, and in the 1950s and 1960s it was a philosophy of waiting. In retrospect both responses of expectation and waiting seem to be justified, even though the expectations were defeated. Though Tillich's work was more in theory, his theory became his primary way of action. It was not a passive philosophy.

Tillich's mentor Ernst Troeltsch wrote often about compromise. Christianity merged with social forces and transformed societies, but in the merging, Christianity was itself transformed. Such was to be the fate of the social thought of Karl Marx in Tillich and in the Western world. The cry of Marx for social ownership and control of industry gradually permeated Western institutions from the Roman Catholic church to the bastions of capitalism in the United States and Western Europe. The more radical demands of the religious socialists were not to be met; however, old laissez-faire capitalism was transformed. It did not become Tillich's theonomous society —a concept also owing much to Troeltsch—but it became a social-welfare capitalism. Republican administrations in the U.S. would call for guaranteed annual incomes under the rubric of a negative income tax, and the Pope would condemn capitalism. On the other hand, groups with only limited access to the structures of power, particularly minorities, would continue to be denied their full right to be. Christian spokesmen for these minorities, such as George Kelsey, Martin Luther King, Jr., and James Cone, would use some of Tillich's ontology to argue for their people. The classical Marxist class analysis would not remain authoritative in Western-style democracies. Its Leninist expression in theories of imperialism did not capture either Tillich's mind or the consensus of social scientists working on international relations. Tillich was essentially correct: social philosophy could neither consent to Marx nor ignore him if it was to understand the contemporary situation. Marx, rather than representing a final stage of analysis of Western society, was the burning stream through which that analysis must pass.

There is always a gap between theory and practice. Christian faith is more easily correlated with socialism in theory than in practice. In practice, the Christian faith has been better protected under structures of capitalism than any structure socialism has produced. It is Christianity's fate to live in the Western world under conditions of modified or social-welfare capitalism. Mixed economies seem to have the capacity to resist consummate tyranny while avoiding the petty tyrannies of economic overlords. A social-welfare capitalism is not the theonomous society, but it may be a stage on the way to a society in which human creativity is given more opportunity for fulfillment than in any alternative we in the West have yet seen.

Tillich's favorite painting, Picasso's "Guernica," expresses the danger of brutalized war and social disintegration that now rests just under the surface of our society. Kafka's *The Castle* illustrates the numbing power that huge bureaucracies wield in denying human fulfillment, and Langston Hughes's "A Dream Deferred" testifies to the rage of minorities denied the human fulfillment promised by the system. For those who are moved to agree with the basic vision of Tillich's radical social thought, the task is to articulate a theory of social reality that finds meaning in Christian faith and that is correlated with social-welfare capitalism. Such a theory also must engender the energy to oppose the present demons of militarism and nuclear war, repressive bureaucracy, and exclusion of groups from opportunity. Such a vision among the heirs of Tillich is finally, of course, another way of saying community, peace, freedom, and equality.

Tillich was primarily a theoretician of practice. Others will have to put the theory into practice and in so doing work out the compromises that practice always demands of theory. The establishment of groups to battle the powers of militarism, bureaucracy, and systematic discrimination for the sake of the fighting Kingdom of God is of the first importance. My hope for this study is that it will be a resource for those groups already existing in church and society and that it will inform social action for the Kingdom of God that is and will be.

Notes

Notes to Chapter 1

1. Renate Albrecht and Gertraut Stöber, "The Places of Tillich's Childhood," *Newsletter of the North American Paul Tillich Society* 2, no. 1 (October, 1975), p. 2.
2. Paul Tillich, *The Interpretation of History*, tr. N. A. Rasetzki and Elsa L. Talmey (New York: Charles Scribner's Sons, 1936), p. 4.
3. See Erik H. Erikson, *Childhood and Society*, 2d ed., rev. and enl. (New York: W. W. Norton, 1963), pp. 247–74.
4. Wilhelm and Marion Pauck, *Paul Tillich: His Life & Thought* (New York: Harper & Row, 1976), vol. 1, *Life*, p. 1.
5. Quoted in Rollo May, *Paulus: Reminiscences of a Friendship* (New York: Harper & Row, 1973), p. 41.
6. Ibid., pp. 39–40.
7. Pauck and Pauck, *Life*, pp. 35–36.
8. S. William Halperin, *Germany Tried Democracy: A Political History of the Reich from 1918 to 1933* (New York: Thomas Crowell, 1946), p. 5.
9. Fritz Stern, *The Politics of Cultural Despair: A Study in the Rise of the Germanic Ideology* (New York: Doubleday, 1965), p. 21.
10. James R. Lyons, ed., *The Intellectual Legacy of Paul Tillich* (Detroit: Wayne State University Press, 1969), p. 101.
11. Thomas Mann, *Doctor Faustus*, tr. H. T. Lowe-Porter (New York: Knopf, 1963), pp. 86–98.
12. James Luther Adams recommends the following book to those interested in Mann's use of Tillich's memorandum: Gunilla Bergsten, *Thomas Mann's* Doctor Faustus: *The Sources and Structure of the Novel*, tr. Krishna Winston (Chicago: University of Chicago Press, 1969).
13. Lyons, *Intellectual Legacy*, p. 105.

14. Ibid.
15. Wilhelm Pauck's analysis of the importance of the Wingolf to Tillich sheds much light on Tillich's own valued memories from his student days. Pauck and Pauck, *Life,* pp. 20–29.

Notes to Chapter 2

1. Paul Tillich, *A History of Christian Thought: From Its Judaic and Hellenistic Origins to Existentialism,* ed. Carl E. Braaten (New York: Simon and Schuster, 1967), p. 438.
2. Paul Tillich, *Gesammelte Werke,* 14 vols. (Stuttgart: Evangelisches Verlagswerk, 1959–75),1:9(hereafter cited as *Gesammelte Werke*).
3. Victor Nuovo, "Translator's Introduction," in Paul Tillich, *The Construction of the History of Religion in Schelling's Positive Philosophy: Its Presuppositions and Principles* (Lewisburg, Pa.: Bucknell University Press, 1974), p. 12.
4. Franz Gabriel Nauen, *Revolution, Idealism and Human Freedom: Schelling, Hölderlin and Hegel and the Crisis of Early German Idealism,* International Archives of the History of Ideas, vol. 45 (The Hague: Martinus Nijhoff, 1971), p. 23.
5. Nuovo, in Tillich, *The Construction,* p. 16. The *me on* is relative nonbeing. That is, it is the potentiality of being in the divine life. It cannot be named directly, and it is the presupposition of thought. It is the element that is ontologically contrasted with pure form. See also Paul Tillich, *Systematic Theology,* 3 vols. (Chicago: University of Chicago Press, 1951–63), 1:179.
6. Tillich, *The Construction,* pp. 52–53.
7. "But this little book [*Christianity and the Encounter of the World Religions*] signifies only the beginning of a new phase in Paul Tillich's thought." Mircea Eliade, "Paul Tillich and the History of Religions," in Paul Tillich, *The Future of Religions,* ed. Jerald C. Brauer (New York: Harper & Row, 1966), p. 32.
8. Paul Tillich, *Christianity and the Encounter of the World Religions* (New York: Columbia University Press, 1963).
9. Tillich, *The Construction,* p. 111.
10. Ibid., p. 127.

11. Ibid., p. 122.
12. Ibid., p. 127.
13. Tillich, *History of Christian Thought,* p. 401.
14. Paul Tillich, *Mysticism and Guilt-Consciousness in Schelling's Philosophical Development,* tr. Victor Nuovo (Lewisburg, Pa.: Bucknell University Press, 1974). There is considerable evidence that this work, published originally in 1912, was dependent on the first dissertation and that Tillich regarded the second work as the more important. It is also probable that the second work was begun first and that the work on the dissertation published in 1910 interrupted the work on the second.
15. Ibid., p. 30.
16. Ibid., p. 31.
17. Ibid., p. 117.
18. Ibid., p. 125.
19. Tillich, *History of Christian Thought,* p. 374.
20. Ibid., p. 384.
21. Tillich, *Mysticism and Guilt-Consciousness,* p. 25.

Notes to Chapter 3

1. Wilhelm and Marion Pauck, *Paul Tillich: His Life & Thought* (New York: Harper & Row, 1976), vol. 1, *Life,* pp. 43–44.
2. Paul Tillich, *Gesammelte Werke,* 13:78.
3. Paul Tillich, "Predigt gehalten nach den Kämpfen bei Tahure am 30. und 31. Oktober, 1915," Tillich Papers, Harvard University Archives, Cambridge, Mass. (hereafter cited as Tillich Papers).
4. Pauck and Pauck, *Life,* p. 49.
5. Tillich, *Gesammelte Werke,* 13:70.
6. Pauck and Pauck, *Life,* p. 52.
7. Paul Tillich, *A History of Christian Thought: From Its Judaic and Hellenistic Origins to Existentialism,* ed. Carl E. Braaten (New York: Simon and Schuster, 1967), p. 501.
8. Tillich, *Gesammelte Werke,* 13:70.

9. See Paul Tillich, *Dynamics of Faith* (New York: Harper & Brothers, 1957).

10. Pauck and Pauck, *Life,* p. 54.

Notes to Chapter 4

1. Paul Tillich, "Aufruf," Tillich Papers. James V. Fisher has written the fullest account of the *Bund Neue Kirche* and Tillich's association with the group in "The Politicizing of Paul Tillich: The First Phase," in John J. Carey, ed., *Tillich Studies: 1975* (Tallahassee: North American Paul Tillich Society, 1975), pp. 27–38.

2. Letter to Tillich, December 12, 1918, Tillich Papers.

3. Steinhauser to Tillich, May 16, 1919, Tillich Papers.

4. Fisher, "Politicizing of Paul Tillich," p. 34.

5. Paul Tillich, *Gesammelte Werke,* 13:154–60. Idem, "Answer to an Inquiry of the Protestant Consistory of Brandenburg," tr. James Luther Adams, *Metanoia* 3 (September, 1971):10.

6. Steinhauser to Tillich, July 12, 1919, Tillich Papers.

7. Günther Dehn, *Die alte Zeit, die vorigen Jahre* (Munich: Chr. Kaiser Verlag, n.d.), pp. 212–13.

8. Tillich, *Gesammelte Werke,* 12:194–99.

9. Paul Tillich, *The Religious Situation,* tr. H. Richard Niebuhr (New York: Henry Holt, 1932), pp. 158–59.

10. John R. Stumme's work on the Kairos Circle is very complete and helpful, *Socialism in Theological Perspective: A Study of Paul Tillich, 1918–1933,* American Academy of Religion Dissertation Series, no. 21 (Missoula, Mont.: Scholars Press, 1978).

Notes to Chapter 5

1. Paul Tillich, *The Protestant Era,* tr. James Luther Adams (Chicago: University of Chicago Press, 1948), p. 32.

2. Ibid., p. 33.

3. Ibid., p. 43.

4. Paul Tillich, *Political Expectation* (New York: Harper & Row, 1971), p. 179.

5. Paul Tillich, *Systematic Theology,* 3 vols. (Chicago: University of Chicago Press, 1951–63), 3:369–72.
6. Ibid., p. 370.
7. Ibid., p. 371.
8. Reprinted in Tillich, *Political Expectation,* pp. 58–88.
9. Ibid., p. 88.
10. Ibid., p. 62.
11. Ibid., p. 76.
12. Ibid., p. 79.
13. Ibid., p. 82.
14. Ibid., p. 88.

Notes to Chapter 6

1. Max Weber, *The Protestant Ethic and the Spirit of Capitalism,* tr. Talcott Parsons (New York: Charles Scribner's Sons, 1930).
2. Paul Tillich, *The Religious Situation,* tr. H. Richard Niebuhr (New York: Henry Holt, 1932), p. xxv.
3. Ernst Troeltsch, *The Social Teaching of the Christian Churches,* tr. Olive Wyon, 2 vols. (London: Allen & Unwin, 1931).
4. Tillich, *Religious Situation,* pp. 22–24.
5. Ibid., p. 7.
6. "Translator's Preface," in Ibid., p. xv.
7. Paul Tillich, "Gläubiger Realismus I" and "Gläubiger Realismus II," in *Gesammelte Werke,* 4:77–106.
8. Paul Tillich, "Realism and Faith," in idem, *The Protestant Era,* tr. James Luther Adams (Chicago: University of Chicago Press, 1948), pp. 66–82.
9. Ibid., p. 66.
10. Ibid., p. 76.
11. Tillich, *Gesammelte Werke,* 12:96.
12. See Paul Tillich, *The Interpretation of History,* tr. N. A. Rasetzki and Elsa L. Talmey (New York: Charles Scribner's Sons, 1936), pp. 77–122.
13. Ibid., p. 85.
14. Ibid., p. 84.

15. See Roy D. Morrison II, "Tillich's Appropriation of Jacob Boehme," in John C. Carey, ed., *Tillich Studies: 1975* (Tallahassee: North American Paul Tillich Society, 1975) for an illuminating inquiry as to the degree of Tillich's dependence on Böhme. Also important is Tillich's "Preface," in John Joseph Stoudt, *Sunrise to Eternity: A Study of Jacob Boehme's Life and Thought* (Philadelphia: University of Pennsylvania Press, 1957).

16. Tillich, *Gesammelte Werke*, 10:100–7. Appropriately chosen as the lead essay in idem, *Political Expectation* (New York: Harper & Row, 1971).

17. Tillich, *Political Expectation*, p. 8.

18. Tillich, *Gesammelte Werke*, 2:175–92.

19. Ibid., p. 184. Author's translation.

Notes to Chapter 7

1. Peter Gay, "Weimar Culture: The Outsider as Insider," *Perspectives in American History* 2 (1968):36.

2. Ibid.

3. Martin Jay, *The Dialectical Imagination: A History of the Frankfurt School and the Institute of Social Research, 1923–1950* (Boston: Little, Brown, 1973), p. 24.

4. Hannah Tillich, *From Time to Time* (New York: Stein and Day, 1973), pp. 141–56.

5. Ibid., p. 149.

6. Max Horkheimer, "Erinnerungen an Paul Tillich," in *Werk und Wirken Paul Tillichs: Ein Gedenkbuch* (Stuttgart: Evangelisches Verlagswerk, 1967), p. 17.

7. Hannah Tillich, *From Time to Time*, p. 155.

8. Horkheimer, *Werk und Wirken*, p. 16.

9. Jay, *Dialectical Imagination*, p. 285.

10. Ibid., p. 88.

11. Ibid., p. 90.

12. Ibid., pp. 102–3.

13. Ibid., p. 111.

14. Herbert Marcuse, *Eros and Civilization: A Philosophical Inquiry into Freud* (Boston: Beacon Press, 1955).
15. Guyton B. Hammond has contributed a very valuable volume, *Man in Estrangement: A Comparison of the Thought of Paul Tillich and Erich Fromm* (Nashville: Vanderbilt University Press, 1965). Unfortunately, it is innocent of any reflection of the impact of the institute on either thinker.
16. Jay, *Dialectical Imagination,* p. 279.
17. Paul Tillich, *Political Expectation* (New York: Harper & Row, 1971), p. 180.
18. Paul Tillich, *The Protestant Era,* tr. James Luther Adams (Chicago: University of Chicago Press, 1948), p. 239. The references are to the original edition. The later edition was abridged, and in the process, the last three chapters, the most limited to the immediate postwar scene and the most socialist, were eliminated.
19. Ibid., p. 240.
20. Ibid.
21. Paul Tillich, "Rejoinder," *The Journal of Religion* 46 (January, 1966):190.
22. Tillich, *Protestant Era,* p. 224.
23. Ibid., p. 260.
24. Ibid., p. 258.

Notes to Chapter 8

1. Paul Tillich, *The Socialist Decision,* tr. Franklin Sherman (New York: Harper & Row, 1977). See "Die sozialistische Entscheidung," in *Gesammelte Werke,* 2:219–365. (Originally published by Alfred Protte, Potsdam, 1933.)
2. Hannah Tillich, *From Time to Time* (New York: Stein and Day, 1973), p. 156.
3. Tillich, *Gesammelte Werke,* 13:177–79.
4. Paul Tillich, *The Religious Situation,* tr. H. Richard Niebuhr (New York: Henry Holt, 1932).
5. In a previous publication of the content of this chapter, I

translated *Widerstreit* as "antagonism." Franklin Sherman's translation as "conflict" is better, and I have adopted it. See Ronald Stone, "Tillich: Radical Political Theologian," *Religion in Life* 46, no. 1 (1977):44–53.

6. Tillich, *Gesammelte Werke*, 2:365.

Notes to Chapter 9

1. Quoted in Beate Ruhm von Oppen, *Religion and Resistance to Nazism* (Princeton: Princeton University Center of International Studies, 1971), p. 9.

2. Quoted in Arthur C. Cochrane, *The Church's Confession under Hitler* (Philadelphia: Westminster Press, 1962), p. 80.

3. Tillich, *Gesammelte Werke*, 13:177–79.

4. Wilhelm and Marion Pauck, *Paul Tillich: His Life & Thought* (New York: Harper & Row, 1976), vol. 1, *Life*, pp. 157–59.

5. Speech before the Conference on Christian German Refugees, Riverside Church, New York City, June 6, 1936. See also Tillich, *Gesammelte Werke*, 13:187–91.

6. James A. Zabel, *Nazism and the Pastors: A Study of the Ideas of Three* Deutsche Christen *Groups,* American Academy of Religion Dissertation Series, no. 14 (Missoula, Mont.: Scholars Press, 1976), p. 22.

7. Paul Tillich, "Die Theologie des Kairos und die gegenwärtige geistige Lage," *Theologische Blätter* 13, no. 11 (1934):305–28.

8. Paul Tillich, "Um was es geht," *Theologische Blätter* 14, no. 5 (1935):117–20.

9. See Walter F. Benze, "Tillich's *Kairos* and Hitler's Seizure of Power: The Tillich-Hirsch Exchange of 1934–35," in John J. Carey, ed., *Tillich Studies: 1975* (Tallahassee: North American Paul Tillich Society, 1975), pp. 39–50.

10. Zabel, *Nazism and the Pastors,* p. 230.

11. Paul Tillich, *My Travel Diary: 1936, Between Two Worlds,* ed. Jerald C. Brauer, tr. Maria Pelikan (New York: Harper & Row, 1970).

12. Ibid., p. 145.

13. Ibid., pp. 42, 85, 105, and 168.
14. Ibid., p. 16.
15. Paul Tillich, "The Kingdom of God and History," in H. G. Wood et al., *The Kingdom of God and History* (London: Allen & Unwin, 1938).
16. Ibid., p. 114.
17. Ibid.
18. Ibid., p. 126.
19. A more complete analysis of the end of the Protestant era is found in Paul Tillich, "The End of the Protestant Era," *The Student World* 30, no. 1 (1937):49–57.
20. Paul Tillich, "The Church and Communism," *Religion in Life* 6, no. 3 (1937):347–57.
21. Ibid., p. 347.
22. Ibid.
23. Ibid.
24. Ibid., p. 350.
25. Ibid., p. 357.
26. Ibid.
27. Paul Tillich, "The Meaning of Anti-Semitism," *Radical Religion* 4, no. 1 (1938):34–36.

Notes to Chapter 10

1. Paul Tillich, "The Gospel and the State," *Crozer Quarterly* 15, no. 4 (1938):251–61.
2. Paul Tillich, "The Political Situation in Europe since the Munich Conference," Tillich Papers.
3. Paul Tillich, "I Am an American," *Protestant Digest* 2, no. 4 (June–July, 1941):24–26. See also idem, "The Conquest of Theological Provincialism," in Franz L. Neumann et al., *The Cultural Migration: The European Scholar in America* (Philadelphia: University of Pennsylvania Press, 1953), pp. 138–56.
4. Paul Tillich, "Protestant Principles," *The Protestant* 4, no. 5 (April–May, 1942):17.
5. *The Protestant* 4, no. 7 (August–September, 1941):8–14.
6. Ibid., p. 14.

7. Paul Tillich, *War Aims* (New York: Protestant Digest, 1941).

8. Paul Tillich, "The Jewish Question: Christian and German Problem," *Jewish Social Studies* 33, no. 4 (1971):261.

9. Paul Tillich, *An meine deutschen Freunde* (Stuttgart: Evangelisches Verlagswerk, 1973), p. 19.

10. Ibid., p. 21.

11. Paul Tillich, "Catholicism and Anti-Judaism" and "Protestantism and Anti-Semitism," Tillich Papers.

12. Tillich, "Catholicism and Anti-Judaism," p. 1.

13. Ibid., p. 7.

14. Tillich, "Protestantism and Anti-Semitism," pp. 11–12.

15. Ibid., p. 12.

16. Paul Tillich, "The God of History," *Christianity and Crisis,* May 1, 1944, pp. 5–6.

17. A sample of a few of the titles of Tillich's messages indicates the integration of politics and theology that characterized his thought: The Jewish Question, Russia's Religious Situation, The Resistance of the Norwegian Church, Book Burning, American Faith in Democracy, Post-war Formation as New Social-Economic Order, Tragedy in the Historical Movement, The Conquest of the Political Immaturity of the German People, The World after the War, The Inner Limits of Power, Advent Hope, Light in the Future Darkness, Ten Years of Hitler, Christianity and German History, Limits of Tyranny, Conditions for a United Europe, Defeat of the New Heathenism, Fascism and National Socialism, Guilt and Atonement, The Fifth War-time Christmas Eve, Justice as Deliverance, The Suffering of Jesus and the Suffering of the German People, and In Expectation of Liberation.

18. Paul Tillich, "Christian Principles and Political Reality," "The Social Problem of a Just and Durable Peace," and "The International Problem of a Just and Durable Peace," Tillich Papers.

19. "A Program for a Democratic Germany," *Christianity and Crisis,* May 15, 1944, pp. 3–5.

20. Paul Tillich et al., *The Christian Answer,* ed. Henry P. Van Dusen (New York: Charles Scribner's Sons, 1945).

21. Tillich, *Gesammelte Werke,* 9:139–92.
22. Reprinted as Paul Tillich, *The World Situation,* Social Ethics Series, no. 2 (Philadelphia: Fortress Press, Facet Books, intro., 1965).
23. Ibid., p. 24.
24. Ibid., p. 26.
25. Ibid., p. 27.

Notes to Chapter 11

1. Wilhelm and Marion Pauck, *Paul Tillich: His Life & Thought* (New York: Harper & Row, 1976), vol. 1, *Life,* p. 205.
2. Paul Tillich, "Beyond the Usual Alternatives," *The Christian Century,* May 7, 1958, p. 554.
3. To be discussed further in the next chapter.
4. John J. Carey, "Morality and Beyond: Tillich's Ethics in Life and Death," in idem, ed., *Tillich Studies: 1975* (Tallahassee: North American Paul Tillich Society, 1975), p. 108.
5. Glenn Graber, "The Metaethics of Paul Tillich," *Journal of Religious Ethics* 1 (Fall, 1973):113.
6. Paul Tillich, "Ethical Principles of Moral Action" (Speech given at Florida State University, Tallahassee, Fla., March 2, 1962).
7. Paul Tillich, "Problems of Christian Ethics" (Speech given in Dallas, Texas, May 28, 1962).
8. Paul Tillich, *Morality and Beyond* (New York: Harper & Row, 1963), pp. 65–81.
9. Paul Tillich, *Love, Power, and Justice: Ontological Analyses and Ethical Applications* (London: Oxford University Press, 1954), p. 25.
10. Paul Tillich, *The Religious Situation,* tr. H. Richard Niebuhr (New York: Henry Holt, 1932).
11. Tillich, *Gesammelte Werke,* 2:91. Reprinted as "Christianity and Modern Society," in idem, *Political Expectation* (New York: Harper & Row, 1971).
12. Paul Tillich, "Man and Society in Religious Socialism," *Christianity and Society* 8, no. 4 (1943): 10–21.

13. Ibid., p. 17.
14. Ibid.
15. For a discussion of Tillich and ontology, see Alistair M Macleod, *Paul Tillich: An Essay on the Role of Ontology in His Philosophical Theology* (London: Allen & Unwin, 1973)
16. Tillich, *Love, Power, and Justice,* p. 56.
17. Ibid., p. 62.
18. Ibid., p. 71.
19. Tillich, *Gesammelte Werke,* 2:193–208.
20. Paul Tillich, "Power and Justice in the Post-War World," Tillich Papers.
21. Tillich, *Love, Power, and Justice,* pp. 38–39.
22. Ibid., p. 40.
23. Ibid., p. 123.
24. *The Christian Conscience and Weapons of Mass Destruction* (New York: Federal Council of Churches in America, 1950), p. 14.
25. Ibid.
26. Paul Tillich, "Correspondence," *Partisan Review* 39, no. 2 (1962):311–12.
27. Ibid., p. 312.
28. Paul Tillich, Typed Ms., Tillich Papers.
29. A comment to his secretary in his own handwriting testifies both to Tillich's support of the immigration reform legislation and to his lack of interest in electoral politics during his last year at the University of Chicago: "Please telegraph my support if you can find out the name of my congressman and senator from Chicago." Tillich Papers.
30. Paul Tillich, "America's Leaders Speak," *The Washington Post,* October 22, 1964.
31. Paul Tillich, *Systematic Theology,* 3 vols. (Chicago: University of Chicago Press, 1957–63), 2:12.
32. Tillich to Bennett, August 18, 1959. Copy in author's collection.
33. His own evolution is well represented in the position: "I do not doubt that the basic conceptions of religious socialism are valid, that they point to the political and cultural way of life by which alone Europe can be built up. But, I am *not* sure that

the adoption of religious-socialist principles is a possibility in any foreseeable future." Paul Tillich, "Beyond Religious Socialism," *The Christian Century,* June 15, 1949, p. 733.

34. Paul Tillich, "Past and Present Reflections on Christianity and Society" [May, 1955], Tillich Papers, p. 1.

35. Ibid., p. 2.

36. Ibid., p. 4.

Notes to Chapter 12

1. Paul Tillich, *A History of Christian Thought: From Its Judaic and Hellenistic Origins to Existentialism,* ed. Carl E. Braaten (New York: Simon and Schuster, 1967), p. 292.

2. Ibid., p. 293.

3. Paul Tillich, *Systematic Theology,* 3 vols. (Chicago: University of Chicago Press, 1951–63), 1:4.

4. Ibid., p. 31.

5. Ibid., p. 5.

6. Ibid., p. 68.

7. Alexander Solzhenitsyn, "The Exhausted West," *Harvard Magazine* 80, no. 6 (July–August, 1978):21–26.

8. Quoted in Tillich, *Systematic Theology,* 1:11.

9. Ibid., p. 99.

10. Ibid., p. 72.

11. Ibid., p. 86.

12. Ibid., p. 117.

13. Ibid., pp. 76, 92–93.

14. Ibid., p. 220.

15. Ibid., pp. 279–86.

16. Ibid., p. 270.

17. Ibid., 2:66, 74, 88.

18. Ibid., p. 59.

19. Ibid 3:283.

20 Ibid., pp. 293–94.

21. Ibid., pp. 356–57.

22. See Paul Tillich, *Christianity and the Encounter of the World*

Religions (New York: Columbia University Press, 1963), pp. 63–74.

23. Tillich, *Systematic Theology,* 3:344.
24. Ibid., p. 346.
25. Ibid., p. 347.
26. Ibid., p. 389.
27. Ibid., p. 391.
28. Paul Tillich, "The Political Meaning of Utopia," in idem, *Political Expectation* (New York: Harper & Row, 1971), p. 180. This essay was originally delivered in 1951 as lectures at the Deutsche Hochschule für Politik in Berlin.
29. Paul Tillich, "The Person in a Technical Society," in John A. Hutchison, ed., *Christian Faith and Social Action* (New York: Charles Scribner's Sons, 1953), pp. 137–53. Reprinted in Gibson Winter, ed., *Social Ethics: Issues in Ethics and Society* (New York: Harper & Row, 1968), pp. 120–38.
30. Tillich, in Hutchison, *Christian Faith,* p. 153.
31. Paul Tillich, "The Effects of Space Exploration on Man's Condition and Stature," in idem, *The Future of Religions,* ed. Jerald C. Brauer (New York: Harper & Row, 1966), p. 51.
32. Paul Tillich, "Frontiers," in ibid., p. 52.
33. Ibid., p. 60.
34. Paul Tillich, "The Jewish Question: Christian and German Problem," *Jewish Social Studies* 33, no. 4 (1971):254–56.
35. Ibid., pp. 255–56.
36. See chapter 10, note 11.
37. Tillich, "The Jewish Question," p. 259.
38. Ibid., p. 265.
39. Ibid., p. 266.
40. Ibid.
41. Ibid., p. 267.
42. Ibid., p. 268.
43. Ibid., pp. 269–70.
44. Ibid., p. 271.
45. Paul Tillich, "My Changing Thoughts on Zionism" (Speech before the Christian-Jewish Colloquy on Israel's Rebirth in the Middle

East, Chicago, Ill., January 21, 1959). The typed manuscript
with Tillich's handwritten corrections is in the Tillich Papers.
46. Ibid., p. 9.
47. An earlier speech on Israel in Berlin in 1953 was not as clearly
    pro-Zionist in its practical aspects as was the 1959 Chicago speech.
    See Paul Tillich, "Nation of Time, Nation of Space," *Land Reborn* 8, no. 1 (1959):4–5.
48. Wilhelm and Marion Pauck, *Paul Tillich: His Life & Thought*
    (New York: Harper & Row, 1976), vol. 1, *Life*, p. 257.
49. Paul Tillich, "On Peace on Earth," in Winter, *Social Ethics*,
    p. 225.
50. Ibid., p. 231.
51. Reprintedas*Christianity and the Encounter of the World Religions*.
52. See Robert W. Wood, ed., "Tillich Encounters Japan," *Japanese
    Religions* 2, nos. 2 and 3 (May, 1961): 48–71; and "Dialogues,
    East and West: Conversations between Paul Tillich and Hisamatsu Shin'ichi," 3 parts, *The Eastern Buddhist*, n.s., 4, no. 2,
    5, no. 2, and 6, no. 2.
53. Tillich, *Future of Religions*, p. 93.
54. Paul Tillich, "Informal Report on Lecture Trip to Japan"
    [Summer, 1960], Tillich Papers.
55. Ibid., p. 3.
56. Paul Tillich, "Spiritual Foundations of Democracy," Tillich
    Papers.
57. Tillich, *Encounter of World Religions*, p. 75.
58. More recent scholarship on Buddhism has located support
    for democracy of which Tillich was unaware. See Donald
    Swearer, "An Understanding of Buddhist Social Ethics" (Schaff
    Lectures, Pittsburgh Theological Seminary, Pittsburgh, Penn.,
    October 17–19, 1977).
59. Hannah Tillich, *From Time to Time* (New York: Stein and
    Day, 1973), p. 219.
60. Paul Tillich, "Autobiographical Reflections," in Charles W.
    Kegley and Robert W. Bretall, eds., *The Theology of Paul Tillich*
    (New York: Macmillan, 1952), p. 13.
61. Note in Tillich's handwriting. Spock to Tillich, May 12,
    1965, Tillich Papers.

Index

Progress, 71
Proletariat, 20, 61, 66, 71, 80, 129, 144, 154
Promised Land, 149
Prophet, 77, 79–80
Prophetic criticism, 90
Prophetic protest, 86, 99
Prophetic religion, 100, 107
Prophetic spirit, 130
Protestant, 7, 8, 52
Protestant churches, 77, 81, 84
Protestant Digest, The, 99–101
Protestant Era, The, 70, 71
Protestant Ethic and the Spirit of Capitalism, The, 55
Protestantism, 57, 61, 78, 85, 94, 113, 140
Protestantism and Anti-Semitism, 103–4
Protestant principle, 115, 121, 135
"Protestant Principles," 99–100
Prussia, 19
Psychoanalysis, 63, 67–68, 139, 144
Psychoanalytic method, 114
Psychology, 68
Psychotherapy, 114

Race, 71
Radical, 8, 37, 40–45, 59, 74
Ragaz, Leonhard, 44
Rathenau, Walter, 48
Realism, 116
Realists, 120
Realpolitik, 19, 57
Reichstag, 47
Reichstag fire, 84
Relativism, 136
Relativity, 119
Religion, 7, 27–29, 43, 52, 55, 81, 82, 100, 152
"Religion and World Politics," 109
Religiöse Lage der Gegenwart, Die (See *The Religious Situation*)
Religious reservation, 52, 53, 88, 95, 144
Religious Situation, The, 50, 55, 109, 154
Religious socialism, 46–53, 55, 61–62, 71, 88–89, 91, 92–93, 95–96, 113, 114, 121, 124, 130, 134, 143–44, 151, 153
Remarque, Erich Maria, 35
Reston, James, 150
Revelation, 28, 89, 133, 136
Revolution, 8, 62, 79, 88, 117
Rhineland, 17
Ribbentrop, Joachim von, 97
Riezler, Kurt, 64
Right wing, 124
Ritschl, Albrecht, 29, 123
Ritschlian, synthesis, 132

Ritschlian theology, 23
Rode, Martin, 44
Röhm, Ernst, 84
Roman Catholic, 16, 155
Romanovs, 19
Romans 13, 141
Romanticism, 135
Rome, 141
Roosevelt, Eleanor, 126
Roosevelt, Franklin D., 98, 112
Ruhr, 19, 48
Rusk, Dean, 150
Russia, 64, 97–98, 106, 141
Rüstow, Alexander, 44

Salvation, 82, 102, 124
Sartre, Jean Paul, 123, 144
Scarlett, William, 107
Schaft, Hermann, 23
Scheidemann, Philipp, 46
Scheler, Max, 54
Schelling, Friedrich, 24–31, 57, 106, 114, 116, 123, 131, 132, 136, 152
Schleiermacher, F.E.D., 28, 131
Schleppfus, Eberhard, 21
Science, 55, 116
2 Corinthians 4:17–18, 33
Seeger, Daniel Andrew, 128
Self, 8, 29, 116–17
Self-Help for Emigrés from Central Europe, 86
Sex, 120
Sexuality, 118
Sexual morality, 117, 127
"Significance of the History of Religions for the Systematic Theologian, The," 151
Sinzheimer, Hugo, 66
Situation, 119
Skepticism, 134
Social Democratic Party (SDP), 19, 39, 41, 46–48, 53, 61, 66, 74, 79, 80
Social ethics, 112–30, 133, 139
Social gospel, 140
Socialism, 20, 40, 42–44, 50, 52, 61–62, 73–82, 85, 153, 155
"Socialism as a Question of the Church," 42
Socialist cause, 120
Socialist Decision, The, 7, 50, 51, 65, 66, 67, 72, 78–82, 84, 102, 142, 154
Socialists, 122
Social philosophy, 8, 9, 15, 17, 30, 109, 113, 133, 135, 139
Social science, 115
Social theology, 137, 144
Social theory, 9, 63, 153